Richard Ashe King

Swift in Ireland

Richard Ashe King

Swift in Ireland

ISBN/EAN: 9783337322335

Printed in Europe, USA, Canada, Australia, Japan

Cover: Foto ©ninafisch / pixelio.de

More available books at **www.hansebooks.com**

SWIFT IN IRELAND

BY

RICHARD ASHE KING, M.A.

Author of "Love the Debt," "The Wearing of the Green,"
etc., etc.

"Εὐεργέτης ἀεὶ ἀναγεγράψῃ."—LUCIAN

London
T. FISHER UNWIN
PATERNOSTER SQUARE

Dublin
SEALY, BRYERS & WALKER
MIDDLE ABBEY STREET

MDCCCXCV

TO MY BROTHER,

DEPUTY SURGEON-GENERAL

HENRY KING,

THIS BOOK IS DEDICATED,

WITH THE AUTHOR'S LOVE.

CONTENTS.

CHAP.		PAGE
I.	SWIFT'S MOTIVES	1
II.	EDUCATION	12
III.	STELLA AND VANESSA	26
IV.	THE ENGLAND OF SWIFT'S DAY	34
V.	IN POWER	54
VI.	THE IRELAND OF SWIFT'S DAY	68
VII.	SWIFT'S FIRST IRISH PAMPHLET	92
VIII.	FIRST "DRAPIER'S LETTER"	105
IX.	FOURTH "DRAPIER'S LETTER"	120
X.	"A MODEST PROPOSAL"	136
XI.	"ON DOING GOOD"	148
XII.	"THE STORY OF THE INJURED LADY"	157
XIII.	MORAL EFFECTS OF OPPRESSION	169
XIV.	SWIFT'S DETRACTORS	180
XV.	"IRELAND IS MY DEBTOR"	195

SWIFT IN IRELAND.

CHAPTER I.

SWIFT'S MOTIVES.

SWIFT drew his first breath and his last in Ireland, spent in her the best years of his youth and of his maturity, owed her his literary education, and paid her with a political education by which she has never ceased to profit to this day; but in no sense was he an Irishman. Indeed, a man less Irish by blood, character, temperament and sympathy it would be hard to point to in Irish history. He came by the father's side of a Yorkshire family, while his mother, as he tells us, was "Mrs. Abigail Erick, of Leicestershire, descended from the most ancient family of the Ericks, who derive their lineage from Erick the forester, a great commander, who raised an army to oppose the invasion of William the Conqueror." It needed Swift's singularity to discover an English ancestor who did not come over with the Conqueror. But if by blood Swift was English of the English, he was more English than the English themselves in his detestation of Ireland. "I happened to be dropped there," he says, "and was a year old before I left it, and to my sorrow did not die before I came back to it." Never once does he use any other tone in speaking of the deplorable accident of his Irish birth. Even in lines jotted down in a note-book which were never meant to see the light, and which, indeed, saw the light at last only lately and by accident, he cries out for the mere relief of his feelings:—

>"Remove me from this land of slaves,
> Where all are fools and all are knaves;
> Where every knave and fool is bought,
> Yet kindly sells himself for naught;
> Where Whig and Tory fiercely fight,
> Who's in the wrong, who in the right;
> And when their country lies at stake,
> They only fight for fighting's sake,
> While English sharpers take the pay,
> And then stand by to see fair play."

And when Swift speaks thus and always thus of Ireland, be it remembered it is of Ireland of the Pale. It is this Ireland alone that he ever even professes to represent. "Our ancestors," he says, "reduced this kingdom to the obedience of England;" and wherever he makes a grudging acknowledgment of being an Irishman at all, it is as one of the English garrison in Ireland. The other and greater Ireland without the Pale he regards sometimes with indifference:—"The Irish Papists are as inconsiderable in point of power as the women and children"—sometimes with fear. "The absentees are in the strongest view our greatest enemies—first, by consuming above one-half of the rents of this nation abroad; and secondly, by turning the weight, by their absence, so much on the Popish side by weakening the Protestant interest"—but generally with a kind of S.P.C.A.

> "Pity for a horse o'er-driven,
> And love in which his hound had part."

And if by blood and in sympathy Swift was an alien, he was yet more un-Irish by temperament and in character. The one characteristic which all students of Celtic history and Celtic genius agree in attributing to the race is what M. Henri Martin describes as its "readiness always to react against the despotism of fact;" while the one characteristic which distinguishes Swift above all writers is the frenzied fury with which he tore off from Nature, from life, and from man every rag, not of ornament only, or only of sentiment, but even of decency, to turn upon them the lurid light of an Inferno.

Yet, un-Irish or even anti-Irish as Swift was by blood, sympathy, character and temperament, Ireland owes him as deep a debt of gratitude for the motives of his immense services to her as for those services themselves. They were not patriotic motives, as I have shown; but neither were they, as most of Swift's biographers assume, malignant motives. Unquestionably they were mixed with political malice in the first years of his championship of our cause and in the first bitterness of his fall from power. When he first feared this fall and felt himself face to face with obscure exile in Ireland, he quoted to Stella the words of Wolsey as ever in his ears :—

"An old man, broken with the storms of state,
Is come to lay his weary bones among ye."

When, however, a little later, he did come an exile to Ireland, he came, not as Wolsey to Leicester, but as Coriolanus to Antium :—

"Now this extremity
Hath brought me to thy hearth—not out of hope—
. . . .
But in mere spite,
To be full quit of those my banishers,
Stand I before thee here. Then, if thou hast
A heart of wreak in thee, that will revenge
Thine own particular wrongs, and stop those maims
Of shame seen through thy country, speed thee straight,
And make my misery serve thy turn; so use it
That my revengeful services may prove
As benefits to thee."

It is not possible to express in closer or apter words the mood of mind which at first stirred Swift to offer Ireland his services for the redress of her grievances. Rage, revenge, dæmonic pride mortified, and baffled party hate at first enlisted him against, not the English, so much as the Whig, misgovernment of Ireland; but, once enlisted, he fought with a higher than mere Swiss loyalty to the flag of his adoption. He never owned, nor did he owe, natural loyalty to Ireland; but he found the Irish flag the fittest in all the world to fight under against the enemies he most hated—cant, baseness, injustice and oppression. Those who maintain that Swift hated these things, not in themselves, but in his political enemies, or in his arch-enemy—human nature—have, I admit, a weighty authority on their side—Swift himself. Such was his horror of the hypocrisy of goodness that he became a kind of devil's hypocrite, and affected a Satanic cynicism amply belied by his private life and by the faithfulness, the affectionateness, the tenderness of his friendships. As with Goldsmith's *Man in Black*, the humanity of his acts are in continual contradiction with the inhumanity of his words, and such shocks of bereavement as disclose to you for a moment the depths of his heart, reveal a more than womanly tenderness. In truth, to judge Swift fairly you must see him in those rare moments when the mask of his devil's hypocrisy is torn roughly off by some trouble. Let me take a case in which you can absolutely see him shamefacedly replacing this mask that the shock of a bereavement had torn off. I shall not take such a shattering blow as his mother's death, or Stella's, or that even of a friend, but only that of a man he had befriended. Hearing that a young fellow named Harrison—a mere protégé of promise, in no sense a friend—lay ill and destitute in mean and lonely London lodgings, he had him removed to the healthier air of Knightsbridge, and hurried hither to him with £100 he had begged and borrowed for his relief. "I took Parnell," he writes, "this morning, and we walked to see poor Harrison. I had the hundred pounds in my pocket. I told Parnell I was afraid to knock at the door; my mind misgave me. I knocked, and his man, in tears, told me his master was dead an hour before. Think what grief this is to me. I went to his mother, and have been ordering things for his funeral, with as little cost as possible, to-morrow at ten at night. Lord Treasurer was much concerned when I told him. I could not dine with the Lord Treasurer nor anywhere else; but got a bit of meat towards evening." But a little later, when he had time to master and to mask his heart, he writes of all his unwearying kindness to the lad as feebleness and folly, and concludes with the cynical resolution—"I shall never have courage again to care for making anybody's fortune."

Now, in estimating Swift's motives for throwing himself into the cause of our country, his continual hypocrisy of inhumanity must not be lost sight of. To call these motives patriotic would be to flatter ourselves, though not to flatter him; for they were higher, or at least broader and deeper than patriotic. "I do profess without affectation," he writes to Pope, "that your kind opinion of me as a patriot, since you call it so, is what I do not deserve; because what I do is owing to perfect rage and resentment, and the mortifying sight of slavery, folly and baseness about me among which I am forced to live." Now, what is all this fury against oppression and corruption and injustice but inverted love of fair and pure and just dealing? It is nothing else. "Do not," he cries furiously to a friend, "Do not the corruptions and villainies of men in power eat into your flesh and exhaust your spirits?" "Well, no; they don't." "No! Why—why—how can you help it, how can you avoid it?"

It is not conceivable of any man that he should hate only for hate's sake; and it is less conceivable of Swift than of most men because of the singular intensity and tenderness of his attachments.

If you would know why he hated you must see how he loved, and then it will not seem to you an untenable paradox that his inhumanity itself sprang out of his humanity, as the tartest vinegar, according to the Italian proverb, is a ferment of the sweetest wine. This is not to deny or to justify the vinegar—the *sæva indignatio* of his epitaph—which was the ruling passion of his life. But, if it cannot be denied or justified, it can be explained on the human principle suggested by Chamfort's aphorism, "Whoso is not a misanthropist at forty can never have loved his kind." Swift's misanthropy, it is true, dates from youth, not middle-age, but a man with his eye and insight and experience is older at twenty than most men at forty; and his experience up to twenty was of a specially souring kind. For a good deal of his sardonic misanthropy he was as little responsible as he was for the miserable circumstances of his birth, of his education, and of his start in life, or for the insane taint in his blood and the pressure upon his brain due to congenital disease. Sam Johnson, a man singularly like Swift in many traits of his character, and in many circumstances of his education, no less than in the natural gloom of his temperament, said once of himself what with more truth might have been Swift's confession:—"I have been mad all my life, sir; at least not quite sane." Here is Addison's first experience of Swift, years before he was to acknowledge him in a Dedication as "the greatest genius of the age." He was astonished by the appearance day after day, in St. James' Coffee House, of a clergyman known as "the mad parson," who entered, laid his hat upon a table, and strode up and down the room, heeding no one in his absorption. He was known to speak only once, and that was to a country gentleman whom he confounded by the abrupt question, "Pray, sir, do you remember any good weather in the world?" "Yes, sir; I thank God I remember a great deal of good weather in my time." "Sir, that is more than I can say. I never remember any weather that was not too hot or too cold, too wet or too dry; but however God Almighty contrives it, at the end of the year 'tis all very well," and with this Swift strode from the house. Had Swift here, like so many young men of genius, been merely challenging attention by eccentricity, surely he would have said something less inept and inconsequent. Though not a sane speech, however, its sentiment of embittered discontent was as characteristic of his temper and of his life as his caged-beast pacing to and fro. It was about this time, as he tells us, not without a Swiftian sneer, that "A person of great honour in Ireland (who was pleased to stoop so low as to look into my mind) used to tell me that my mind was like a conjured spirit that would do mischief if I would not give it employment." We all know what happens when a spirit of this sort is turned in upon itself. Trench somewhere remarks upon the significance of the etymology of English words for enjoyment—diversion, distraction, transport, rapture, ecstasy, &c., &c.—all meaning to be taken out of yourself. Conversely, being driven in upon yourself disposes you to melancholy and to misanthropy, and to become a " rogue elephant " to your species. Now Swift, in all the impressionable years of his life—in his childhood, boyhood, youth and early manhood—was driven in upon himself. He had no home and no intimates: a dependant in his boyhood upon the grudging bounty of an uncle, and in his manhood upon the fitful and oppressive patronage of Temple; he was sensitively solitary, and this shrinking solitariness tended in him, as in an animal driven apart from the herd, to savageness.

Have you not here in the taint of insanity in his blood, in his congenital disorder, *labyrinthine vertigo,* which caused such pressure upon his brain, in the gloomy circumstances of his birth seven months after his father's death, and in the bitter and solitary years of his dependent youth, some explanation and extenuation of his misanthropy?

Anyway, the ordinary explanation—a bad heart—shows at once an ignorance of the stuff of which misanthropists are made and of the stuff of which Swift specially was made. Timon's disease is not a black, but a broken heart; while black-hearted men cannot even hate enthusiastically. They can sneer only, and their sneer is cold as the light on graves; but Swift's fury poured from a heart hot within him and convulsed with volcanic agonies. In truth his hatred was but the shadow of his love; and as shadows are darkest where the lights are most intense, so you find, what a knowledge of human nature would lead you to expect, that Swift loved as profoundly as he hated. But while, with that odd inverted hypocrisy which characterised him, he hid away his love as something sinful or shameful, his hate he paraded with a Pharisaic ostentation.

While, then, we must exclude patriotism from the motives of Swift's Irish crusade, we must reckon among them a love which, if not higher than that of country, is deeper and wider—a love of liberty, probity and justice. The filthy ferment of post-revolutionary politics was nowhere anything like so foul as in Ireland; and Swift's gorge rose at it, not the less because it was Whig, though not merely because it was Whig, and he "created here a soul under the ribs of death" through his own intense hatred of tyranny, injustice and corruption.

CHAPTER II.

EDUCATION.

ITH unconscious Shandean humour, Swift, in his fragment of an autobiography, says of himself, "He felt the consequences of the indiscreet marriage of his parents, not only through the whole course of his education, but during the greatest part of his life." A moderate estimate, it will be admitted, of the consequences of one's parents, marriage. But Swift drops here the graver count against his parents for having produced him at all, and arraigns them only for having improvidently produced him. His horror of improvident marriages, which affected disastrously, I think, his own whole life, was natural and inevitable, since there was hardly a day of all his impressionable years which did not give him

bitter reason to reflect upon the consequences to himself of the destitution in which his father's early death left his mother. Two years after his marriage, and seven months before the birth of his great son, Jonathan Swift, the elder, died, leaving his widow to look where she could for the support of herself and her two children. All we know of Swift's mother is his deep love for her; his character of her at her death :—" I have now lost my barrier between me and death ; God grant I may live to be as well prepared for it as I confidently believe her to have been ! If the way to Heaven be through piety, truth, justice and charity, she is there," and this pleasant anecdote, which suggests that her piety was consistent with a whimsical humour :—On one of her rare visits to Dublin to see her son, then in Trinity, she bound over her landlady to keep the delicate secret of an amour with a gentleman, who was to be admitted with due mystery into her lodgings whenever he called. He called daily, and the romantic landlady assisted for weeks, with much bustle and diplomatic finesse, at these assignations before Mrs. Swift informed her that their hero was her son ! Swift, who tells this story of his mother, showed his usual grateful sense of faithful service by appointing this landlady, Mrs. Brent, to be his housekeeper in after years in the deanery, where she figures under the nickname of " Walpole," and where at her death she was succeeded by her daughter, Mrs. Ridgeway. This instance of Swift's gratitude is worth casual mention in connection with his complaint that "he felt the consequences of the indiscreet marriage of his parents through the whole course of his education." This is not the first, nor the last, nor the most bitter reflection Swift makes upon the grudging charity of his uncle Godwin, to which he owed his maintenance at Kilkenny School and in Trinity College, and these recurring complaints have been cited by biographer after biographer in support of the charge of ingratitude reported to have been publicly made at a Visitation dinner against Swift by the Archdeacon of Dublin. At this dinner Dr. Whittingham is said to have shouted across the table at Swift this intentionally exasperating question, "Pray, Mr. Dean, was it not your uncle Godwin who educated you?" Swift disregarded the attack until the question was reiterated so often and so loudly that he was forced to notice it. "Yes, he gave me the education of a dog!" "Then," retorted Whittingham, "you have not the gratitude of a dog!" Now, in the first place, it does not make for the truth of this story that the Dean and the Archdeacon remained, as they did unquestionably, fast friends after this public encounter. But to admit its truth is not to admit the charge of ingratitude it makes against Swift. Why should a man show a dog's gratitude for a dog's treatment? "The dog," says a Portuguese proverb, "wags his tail, not for you, but for your bread;" but with a man it is the hand, and not the bread, which evokes gratitude—not what you give, but how you give it. If Swift were given to the not unnatural ingratitude of a proud man for irrepayable benefits, he would not speak with such warmth of the goodness to him of this uncle's eldest son, nor would he distinguish another uncle, to whom he owed much, as "the best of his relations." It is odd, too, that those biographers who charge Swift with ingratitude admit him to have been the faithfullest of friends, as though an ingrate could be a friend at all. I do not think there can be a doubt that Swift, in all the sensitive and impressionable years of his life, felt the full bitterness of what Dante, in the most pathetic passage in all poetry, perhaps, puts as a prophecy in the mouth of an ancestor:—

"Tu proverai si come sa di sale
Lo pane altrui, e com' è duro calle
Lo scender e salir per l'altrui scale."

"Thou shalt be taught how salt is the savour of the bread of others; how hard the task of climbing and descending the stranger's stairs."

But what were the "consequences" of this dependence or of its consciousness, which, he says, he felt throughout the whole course of his education? Morally, we know they made, or helped to make him a pessimist and misanthropist, but they had, he tells us, also a benumbing mental effect. "He was admitted," he says of himself, "into the University of Dublin, a pensioner, on the 24th April, 1682, where, by the ill-treatment of his nearest relations, he was so discouraged and sunk in his spirits that he too much neglected his academic studies, for some parts of which he had no great relish by nature, and turned himself to reading history and poetry, so that, when the time came for taking his degree of Bachelor of Arts, although he had lived with great regularity and due observance of the statutes, he was stopped of his degree for dulness and insufficiency, and at last hardly admitted in a manner little to his credit, which is called in that College *speciali gratiâ*, on the 15th February, 1685, with four more on the same footing; and this discreditable mark, as I am told, stands upon record in their College registry." It also stands there on record how Swift did at this degree examination:—"Physics—*male*. Greek and Latin—*bene*. Thema (Latin Essay)—*negligenter*."

In truth, the most effective of Swift's teachers was his first—an old nurse who kidnapped him when a year old to carry him off to her native town, Whitehaven, where she kept him till he was three. Hearing that a relative from whom she expected a legacy was dying, she reconciled her duties to this gentleman, to herself, and to her infant charge, by carrying off the baby surreptitiously to Whitehaven, where Mrs. Swift was fain to let him stay in her dread of the effect of the formidable sea-passage of that day upon so young a child. To this nurse, then, belongs the distinction of being the only one of Swift's teachers who found him or made him a promising pupil; since she taught him so early and so well, that at three he could read any chapter in the Bible. Perhaps, though, I am doing an injustice to Kilkenny School, which in this generation had the unique distinction of turning out three men, each supreme in his own walk—Congreve, Swift, and Berkeley. This famous school, which Swift entered at six and quitted for Trinity at fourteen, may have found or made more of their pupil than the University of Dublin discovered. It could hardly have found or made less. The sole distinction he achieved in Trinity, according to a contemporary, who afterwards became its Provost, was that of a charwoman! "Dr. Baldwin had an utter aversion to Dean Swift because he was a Tory, and used to say scornfully of him, that he was remarkable for nothing else, while in college, except for making a good fire. He would not, he said, allow the college woman to do it, but took that trouble on himself." Only the head of an University, I fancy, could be so wooden as to think this story convicted, not himself, but Swift, of

c

stupidity. "No man," says Goethe, "is a hero to his valet, because a valet is capable only of estimating the high and low as they are manifested in the persons of valets." Only an old woman could have discovered in Jonathan Swift only an old woman's cleverness. However, I do not mention this silly saying in support of what I suppose none will question—that an University course is as little likely to discover or develop a genius as a circus is likely to recognise or produce a Pegasus. It is designed not for the encouragement, but for the suppression of originality of any kind; and Swift's originality which consists of stripping all things bare to the bone, was little likely to be appreciated by Fellows and Professors, who dealt only in cast off clothes. My real reason, however, for quoting Dr. Baldwin's fatuous story is the indirect contradiction it gives to the hundred times reiterated charges against Swift of being a rebel within the University and a roué without. We owe these charges partly, perhaps, to an idea that Swift ought to have been a rebel in Dublin, because his temper and circumstances were those that made Sam Johnson a rebel in Oxford. "Ah! sir," he confesses to Boswell, "I was mad and violent. It was bitterness that they mistook for frolic. I was miserably poor, and I thought to fight my way by my literature and wit; so I disregarded all power and all authority."

With this prepossession the rolls and records of Trinity have been examined, and Swift has been confounded with his cousin and namesake, and also with another contemporary who was expelled for lampooning the college authorities. But if Swift's own assertion, "I lived there with great regularity and due observance of the statutes," is to be discredited—and a more scrupulously truthful man never lived—surely credit must be given to such an *advocatus diaboli* as Dr. Baldwin? Would this virulent political antagonist have brought up against Swift only the charge of being an old woman, if any other could have been recalled to his discredit? Swift was himself so hard a hitter, and was so indiscreet and indiscriminate in his choice of the persons and things he attacked, that he was assailed from all sides and with charges of all kinds; and a biographer who wishes to be merely just to him must be prepared to fight almost every inch of his ground. The present Provost, Dr. Salmon, the worthiest the University has yet had, has looked into the evidence and satisfied himself that "Swift's shortcomings were not very great, and were due to his confining his studies to subjects which interested himself, neglecting some parts of the prescribed curriculum." Swift's sole college distinction for good or evil, then, was his skill in lighting a fire, and this also is the distinction to which the author of the "Drapier's Letters" owes his place among Irish benefactors. But he had a long apprenticeship to serve before he became a political power either in England or Ireland, and this apprenticeship was served under a competent master, Sir William Temple. Let us see for a moment how he came to learn under Temple's roof that scorn for the back-stairs of statesmanship which was one day to stand Ireland in good stead. Even in an early ode to Temple himself he expresses it:—

> "The wily shafts of state, those juggler's tricks,
> Which we call deep designs and politics.
> . . . .
> How plain I see through the deceit!
> How shallow, and how gross the cheat!"

An odd incident was the occasion, if not the cause of a resolution which decided the course of Swift's life. As he stood one day looking gloomily out of the windows of his rooms upon the college quadrangle, troubled about his debts and difficulties, and despondent about his prospects, he saw a sailor evidently out of his bearings, looking perplexedly round the court. If only he had come with supplies from his cousins, who were settled as merchants in Lisbon! He had. He found, at last, Swift's rooms, and poured out from a bag the gold the Lisbon cousins had trusted him with for the distressed student. Nothing would induce the honest tar to take a farthing for his trouble and his trustworthiness, though Swift pressed upon him a larger sum than he was ever again likely to press upon a similar commissionaire. For, from that hour, he tells us, dated two resolutions—which at bottom were one—of independence and of economy. He would never again draw upon his cousins, and he would henceforth be rigid in his economy and in his accounts. Here again, let me say in passing, Swift's detractors have found a text and theme for their attacks. Even Johnson sneers at "the passion which seems to have been deeply fixed in Swift's heart—the love of a shilling." What Swift loved was, not a shilling, but independence; as he writes to Pope: "Wealth is liberty." If he loved a shilling in the sordid sense of Johnson's sneer, how happens it that few more generous men than Swift ever lived? I have before me now an account of his expenditure for the year 1700, and I find from it that nearly one-sixth of a narrow income went in charity. And when he grew older and his income larger—when, that is, not age only but increasing means (*Crescit amor nummi quantum ipsa pecunia crescit*) ought to have hardened habit into avarice, Sheridan tells us that he lived on a third of his income, gave a third away, and saved a third for posthumous charity. Swift loved a shilling only as he hated the bitter dependence and the stinging memory of that dependence, to which the lack of a shilling subjected him in the most sensitive years of his life.

Whether Swift's resolution of independence would have set him to seek an opening in Ireland I cannot say, for the breaking out of the Revolution drove him to England and to his mother's home in Leicester. Here, after some time and debate, it was decided to apply for employment to Sir William Temple. Mrs. Swift could claim relationship to Lady Temple—the Dorothy Osborne whose love-letters have all the charm of the best papers in the *Spectator*—while Swift could plead a family friendship between Sir William's father and his uncle Godwin. Therefore they applied to Temple with some confidence and successfully; and towards the close of 1689 Swift entered on his undefined, and therefore unsatisfactory, duties in the Temple household. When you do not know your precise position you are pretty sure, in such a household, of some hard knocks in groping about to find it. Hence it is not surprising that Swift's first stay with Sir William Temple—in the capacity rather of an amanuensis than of a secretary—was not pleasant and was not long. Having entered Sir William's service at the close of 1689, he quitted it in May of the following year (under the pretext of returning to Ireland for his health) with such a letter from that superior person as proves that in all these months he never once "was pleased to stoop so low as to look into the mind" of his dependent. In this letter Temple recommends Swift to the Secretary of the Irish Viceroy as a suitable person either as "an amanuensis or as a Fellow of Dublin University," since "he has Latin and Greek, some French, and writes a very good current hand; is very honest and diligent." Here Sir William, who was nothing if not a diplomatist, takes strategic care to cover all the ground. If cleverness, French, and a good hand could not secure Swift the post of amanuensis, then Latin and Greek ought at least to gain the plucked degree candidate a Fellowship. Honesty and diligence are thrown in as a makeweight for either scale. Yet Swift never obtained even the Fellowship, though there is extant evidence that he did really write a good current hand; and after a year and a half's sojourn in Dublin and Leicester in vain search for another opening, he returned at the close of 1691 to the Temple household. A year and a half of rough experience must have taught much to a man of Swift's age and of his insight, and may have taught even him humility. Only lowliness on Swift's part could invite a personage so exalted as Sir William "to stoop so low as to look into his mind"—as Temple certainly did during this second visit. "Growing into some confidence with Sir William," Swift writes of himself, "he was often trusted with matters of great importance"—of no less importance, indeed, in one instance, than a commission to convey his patron's views on the proposed Triennial Bill to King William. Swift seems to have been under the singular impression that his knowledge of history on a purely historical question would suffice to convert to Temple's views such a Philistine as King William, and the failure of his mission, therefore, was, he says, "the first incident that helped to cure him of vanity." On the other hand, his Majesty repaid Swift's historical lesson by teaching him to cut asparagus in the Dutch fashion, a favour which I hope made up to Swift for the King's failure to fulfil his promise to him of a prebend of Canterbury or Westminster. For an offer from Sir William Temple to him of a post in the Irish Rolls Office, of the value of £120 a year, having overcome Swift's scruple to enter the Church merely for a maintenance, he had at last resolved to take orders. It was with this view that, through Sir William's influence, he had obtained an *ad eundem* Oxford degree in June, 1692, and a month later had become an M.A. of that University. It was not, however, till 1694 that Swift, despairing at last of the promised English prebend, made his mind up to take orders in Ireland. Sir William's remissness (probably due to his sense of the value of Swift's services as secretary) to use his influence to procure the promised preferment was the cause of their parting, for the second time, in coolness, if not in anger. If Temple felt aggrieved by the defection, or by its cause, or by its manner, he had a revenge which would have satisfied any man, however vindictive. The Irish bishops required a certificate of good conduct during the years which had intervened since Swift's graduation in Trinity, and such a certificate could be obtained only from Sir William. The abjectness of Swift's letter of application for it is at once pitiful and piteous; for how must a white sheet of such penitence have burned a man of Swift's pride like a shirt of Nessus! Temple's reply, returning the desired testimonial, made way for a reconciliation; and Swift, soon tiring of the savage solitude of Kilroot —the little Irish living to which he had been ordained —returned for the third time to Moor Park in May, 1696. It is from this third residence with Temple that Swift's political activity dates; but before I proceed to treat of his politics, and of the secret of the aim and of the reach of his political power, I must, in passing, say a word on what has been called, I think unnecessarily, "the mystery of his life."

CHAPTER III.

STELLA AND VANESSA.

HEN Swift was about thirty years of age he wrote down a memorandum of resolutions headed:— "When I come to be old"—which was found in his desk after his death. In his desk after death was found also a scrap of paper enclosing a lock of hair with an inscription which might have been written in "the ruddy drops that visited his sad heart" —"Only a Woman's Hair." Is there not the connection between this inscription and the fifth of these old-age resolutions that there is between the epilogue and the prologue of a tragedy? This fifth resolution runs thus: "Not to be fond of children, or let them come near me hardly." How shortsighted the recoil

of some of Swift's biographers from this resolution as inhuman! It is human as Hamlet's wild and whirling indictment of Ophelia for inspiring him with love. All the other resolutions are against weaknesses he felt or feared. Is this the sole exception? Surely he would need to make no resolution against a natural antipathy? I have myself no doubt that this resolution which comes in so incongruously among the rest, was suggested, not indeed by what he feared in the future, but by what he felt in the present—the fatal hold Esther Johnson in her childhood and through her childishness had taken on his heart. Esther, the elder of two daughters of the widow of a confidential servant of Sir William Temple's, was eight years of age when Swift first came to reside in the same household with her. Swift undertook her education, and found her an apt, a winning, and an adoring pupil. A proud man's love is always drawn out by the benefits he confers rather than by those he receives, and Swift of all men must have found the relief immense at Moor Park to play for some hours daily the part of an adored patron in place of that of a slighted dependent. Again, Swift, the most masterful of men, made always that oriental submissiveness exacted from childhood, a preliminary and indispensable condition—with the sex—of his friendship. The rules ordaining this and other oriental observances, which he formulated in jest, he insisted

on seriously, with the result which might be expected
—the adoration of the sex

> "That seeks to find in those they love,
> Stern strength and promise of control."

Now Stella's submissiveness, dating from childhood, was naturally childlike to the close of her life. Her worship of Swift was also childlike in its implicitness, while it ripened with years into a woman's passion; and this devotion he returned with a love as tender and intense as a man ever felt for a woman. I do not envy the man who is untouched by the infantile prattle of *The Journal to Stella*—written in the intervals of his dictating the policy of England at home and abroad—or who is unmoved by the white-hot agony of his anxiety during her illness or of his anguish after her death. Yet he marries her—if indeed he married her at all—only late in life and then only in form. Why? This is what is called "the mystery" of his life, which the ingenuity of a host of biographers has been taxed to explain. Some account for it by the suggestion that Swift and Stella were brother and sister—illegitimate children of Sir William Temple's by different mothers—a suggestion which hardly needed the demonstrative evidence that has been adduced to disprove it; since the mere marriage form itself seems to me to disprove it. If one must needs find a mystery in Swift's life, then there is one infinitely more unaccountable to readers of *A Tale of a Tub* than his merely formal marriage to Stella—the mystery of his sincere and supreme faith in the Church of England. That a man who saw everything with so piercing an eye and in so fierce a light as Swift did, could not see that in *A Tale of a Tub* he had dug the foundations of his Church away, is to me far and away the most inexplicable mystery of his life. However, there is no doubt at all that he did really and entirely believe in his Church; and to such a believer it would have seemed sacrilege to go through the form of an incestuous marriage.

But this discredited theory has been displaced in later biographies by another no less unwarrantable— Swift's constitutional incapacity of love. But how is this theory reconcilable with his Leicester flirtations in general, and specially that with Miss Betty Jones, which so alarmed his mother, who probably knew something of his temperament? How is it reconcilable with the vehement passion of his proposal to Miss Waring ("Varina")? Or how even with his original intention to marry Stella the moment he was in a position to maintain a wife? What less than such an intention do these words, coming from a man so scrupulously sincere as Swift, express? "I beg you to be easy," he writes from London to her, "I beg you to be easy till fortune takes her course, and to believe that your felicity is the great goal I aim at in all my pursuits."

If Swift might have married Betty Jones, would have married "Varina," and meant to marry Stella, I think this second theory can be accepted only in default and in despair of any other adequate explanation.

But surely we have an adequate explanation in the two horrors which haunted Swift's life—horror of poverty and dependence in his youth, and horror of impending madness in his manhood? Over and over again he inveighs against the weakness and wickedness of improvident marriages. Here is a Swiftian parable wherewith he poured in oil and wine into the wounds of a hapless curate, who had made such a marriage:—"When I was a schoolboy at Kilkenny, and in the lower form, I longed very much to have a horse of my own to ride on. One day I saw a poor man leading a very mangy, lean horse out of the town to kill him for his skin. I asked the man if he would sell him, which he readily consented to do, upon my offering him somewhat more than the price of his hide, which was all the money I had in the world. I immediately got on him to the great envy of some of my school-fellows, and to the ridicule of others, and rode him about the town. The horse soon tired, and lay down. As I had no stable to put him into, nor any money to pay for his sustenance, I began to find out what a foolish bargain I had made, and cried heartily for the loss of my cash; but the horse dying soon after upon the spot, gave me some relief." I ought to add that when the curate with tears admitted that this romantic parable fitted every circumstance of his case, Swift interested himself successfully to procure his promotion.

When, however, Swift had himself obtained such promotion as would have enabled him to maintain a wife in comfort, he had become haunted with the spectre of a more frightful presentiment. It was not often that Swift disclosed his deepest feelings even to his dearest friends, and it must have been the overpowering pressure of this horror which impelled him to open his heart to its blackest depth one day to Young, the poet, "I shall die at the top, like that tree!" His uncle, Godwin, had died so, and there must, I think, have been a brooding consciousness in his mind that the nickname of "mad parson" by which he was known both in London and in Ireland in his youth, was not given without ground. But chiefly the increase in the violence of the attacks of the congenital disease, *Labyrinthine Vertigo*, which caused not only dizziness and deafness, but intolerable agony and those epileptic seizures which did at last produce paralysis of the brain, warned Swift of his ever-impending doom. Hence this cry of despair to Young; hence his setting aside a third of his income to the sympathetic object of founding an asylum after his death; and hence also, I have no doubt at all, his horror of any marriage not purely formal.

As for the other factitious mystery of his life, his relations to Vanessa, it is precisely as mysterious as Desdemona's love for Othello. If ever there was "a round unvarnished tale delivered" of the whole course of a matter of the kind, it is told in *Cadenus and Vanessa;* and this tale, remember, was not only written solely for Vanessa's eye, but was published solely by Vanessa's vindictive wish. Therefore it is as certain as anything well can be that Swift in *Cadenus and Vanessa* has extenuated nothing against himself, and has set down naught in malice against Vanessa. On the contrary, every line of the poem shows—as it naturally and almost necessarily would show since it was written for her sole reading—a wish to save her self-respect by explaining or extenuating her passionate advances. She makes these advances because :—

> "Two maxims she could still produce,
> And sad experience taught their use:
> That virtue, pleased by being shown,
> Knows nothing which it dares not own;

> Can make us without fear disclose
> Our inmost secrets to our foes;
> That common forms were not designed
> Directors to a noble mind."

On the other hand, she had misread Swift's feelings:—

> "That innocent delight he took
> To see the virgin mind her book
> Was but the master's secret joy
> In school to hear the finest boy."

And she had misread his temperament:—

> "Her scholar is not apt to learn:
> Or wants capacity to reach
> The science she designs to teach:
> Wherein his genius was below
> The skill of every common beau,
> Who, though he cannot spell, is wise
> Enough to read a lady's eyes,
> And will each accidental glance
> Interpret for a kind advance."

If this account of their relations had been written by Swift for publication, or if it had been posthumously published by his executors, something might be said for the charge that it is inaccurate, or imperfect, or unfair to Vanessa; but as Vanessa alone was meant to see it, and as she alone was responsible for its publication, it cannot be suspected of vindicating him unchivalrously at her expense.

CHAPTER IV.

THE ENGLAND OF SWIFT'S DAY.

HE gross misrepresentation of Swift's political principle and principles by that brilliant historical novelist, Macaulay, and others compels me to preface what I have to say on this subject by an account of the incoherent condition of post-revolutionary parties.

Bacon somewhere says that if man had the ordering of the stars he would have arranged them with geometrical symmetry, and historians generally, but particularly partisan historians, are given to such a symmetrical grouping and massing of men and motives, as can nowhere be found outside their pages. Least of all must you look for this chess-board arrangement of sharply defined squares, fixed moves and contrasted colours after the earthquake of a revolution has shifted not old landmarks only but the very land itself. Yet you will find men to write as though Whig and Tory represented before and after the Revolution, and to-day precisely the same principles respectively! Did they represent the same principles respectively even at the same time, but in different countries? To take Swift's political pole-star—his Church—would not a man who was a churchman before all things be with equal sincerity and even vehemence a Whig in Ireland, where the Revolution meant the supremacy of the Church, and a Tory in Scotland, where the Revolution meant the overthrow of the Church? But leaving Ireland and Scotland out of the question and confining ourselves to England, what a kaleidoscope in the hand of fortune were English politics of that day! In the first place, men turned sincerely Whig or Tory according to the chances of a Jacobite restoration. According to these chances you see England more than once, like an unballasted ship with her cargo in bulk, heel suddenly and completely over to one side or the other. But, besides, the issues and interests were at times so confusing and even conflicting that Whigism and Toryism were often to be found mixed inextricably together in the same Englishman, and even in the same English minister. In the same cabinet they were yoked together regularly. Let us see how this came to pass.

It was not the change of dynasty or of the religion

of the dynasty that essentially constituted the Revolution of 1688, but the Bill of Rights which vested the sole right to tax the nation in the House of Commons. This sole right, when supplemented by a resolution of the House to grant supplies to the Crown, only and always annually, made the Commons virtually supreme. Henceforth it was impossible for any English sovereign to oppose or to dispense with the House of Commons for any time, since for that time supplies for the army, for the navy, and for the civil service were obtainable only by the consent of this Chamber. But, on the other hand, the ministers who had the charge and conduct of public business, were the King's servants, appointed by him alone, responsible to him alone, and dismissible only by him. There were indeed two or three indirect means by which the House of Commons could force the King to dismiss a minister; but there were no means direct or indirect, by which it could force the King to appoint a successor more amenable to its control. Hence, a difficulty like that De Quincey humourously describes as embarrassing the Emperor of China upon his first ride in a state-coach presented to him by George III. As such an article had never before been seen in the Celestial Empire, a cabinet council was called to decide the perplexing question, "Where was the Emperor to sit?"

As the hammer-cloth was unusually gorgeous, and the box was beyond question nearest the moon, it was unanimously decided that here was the imperial throne. Accordingly amid a blare of trumpets and the acclaim of all Pekin, the Emperor solemnly ascended to the box seat, with a Minister of State on either side, to the inexpressible delight of everyone, save the English coachman. "But where am I to sit?" he persisted in asking vexatiously until the Privy Council, incensed by his disloyalty, opened the coach-door and bundled him inside. It was the most honourable place certainly, and the proper place for the real master, but—how drive from thence? This, also was the difficulty of the House of Commons, with the King and his Ministers on the box-seat, yet unable to drive, while, though entitled to drive, the Chamber was unable to get at the reins. It was some time before a way out of this *impasse* was discovered, and the discovery was appropriately made by an expert in the extrication of himself out of political difficulties. Robert, Earl of Sunderland, had been a minister of that wretched French-kept creature, Charles II., and had retained his post under his successor by apostatising from Protestantism, until he found it to be his interest to sell James to William as he had sold his faith and country to James. To William he did the service of inventing that patent crank-action of the British Constitution which enables the House of Commons circuitously to work the wheels of the machine. Choose your ministers, he suggested, exclusively from the members of the majority in the House of Commons, and the problem is solved. Thus the King might choose the driver, but the Commons chose the road.

It was some time, however, before William had forced home to him the one effective argument in support of the scheme. It might suit the country and the Commons, but would it suit himself and the one object he had at heart, which was certainly not the suiting of the Commons or the country? Like Charles II. before him and the Georges after him, he regarded England but as the handmaid of a foreign Power, and subordinated her interests, so far as he dared, to this Power's advantage. His heart was in Holland, and in the Grand Alliance of Holland, England, Spain, Austria, and Savoy, against France. His feeling, therefore, towards the two English parties which unsteadied or fettered his foreign policy was "A plague o' both your houses!" until the Whigs—the war party—happened to have a majority in the Commons. When, however, the will of the majority of the House happened to coincide with his own, William hailed Sunderland as a "wise Daniel" and adopted his suggestion to choose his Ministry exclusively from the party of the majority. Henceforth the cabinet was homogeneous and the majority in the House, from being a lawless, reckless, mischievous mob, became an organized and disciplined army. But up to this cabinets had represented, not a party, but the nation, being composed of both Whigs and Tories, who owed loyalty neither to each other nor to the House, but only to the sovereign. Here, then, to begin with, is a difference of coherence and of mutual loyalty between the parties of that day and ours, which is left out of account by those who charge Swift with interested and cynical political apostasy.

But, again, the issues were so intermixed that every Whig had something in him of a Tory and every Tory something in him of a Whig, which a change in the ever-shifting political situation might bring to the top. For instance, the loyalty of the vast majority of the nation to William was of the precise kind O'Connell defined his to the Whig party to be :—" I support the Whigs," he said, "for the same reason that the Kerry omedhaun stuck his hat into a broken pane—not to let in the light, but to keep out the rain." Similarly the sullen Dutchman, who accepted the English throne as a man marries a rich, but repellent woman for the fortune he needs to carry on a law suit with a neighbour, owed most of such loyalty as he commanded, not to letting in the light, but to keeping out the rain—to standing between the country and James. No nurse-maid's bogey was ever more effective to frighten nervous children into obedience than the horror of James's restoration was to cow Englishmen into loyalty to William. Thus a French victory, dread of a French invasion, or the acknowledgment by Louis of the Pretender, made multitudes of Tories sound Whigs for the nonce; while, on the other hand, when this fear had subsided, like a flood which had driven together to a common refuge creatures usually at war, other motives emerged to make sound, *ci-devant* Whigs sincerely zealous Tories. The Church in danger, or danger to the landed interest, or the pressure of taxation, or the destruction of English commerce by the privateers of France, would carry the country with a rush over to the Tory side.

But to come down from these generalities to Swift's attitude towards the particular political personages and parties with which he had to deal, let me put first, not in order only, but also in importance, his idea of party allegiance. In his first political pamphlet, "On the Dissensions at Athens and Rome," he makes a protest against party government which he never lost an opportunity of repeating with even greater emphasis all his life long:—"Because Clodius and Curio happen to agree with me in a few singular notions, must I therefore, blindly follow them in all? . . . Is it not possible that on some occasion Clodius may be, bold and insolent, borne away by his passion, malicious and revengeful? That Curio may be corrupt, and expose to sale his tongue and his pen. I conceive it far below the dignity of human nature and human reason to be engaged in any party, the most plausible soever, upon such servile conditions." It hardly needed, however, his own repeated protestations to assure us that Swift, *nullius addictus jurare in verba magistri*, was the last man in the world to bind himself blindly and implicitly to any party. The Whigs represented his State politics, the Tories represented his Church policies; when the State seemed to him secure against Jacobitism, and the Church seemed to him in danger from Whiggery, he maintained his consistency by changing his side. Let me make this clear by epitomizing the political history of the years between the publication of this Whig pamphlet, "On the Dissensions at Athens and Rome," and Swift's support in *The Examiner* of the Tories.

"The Dissensions at Athens and Rome," the first of Swift's political tracts, was written when the extreme unpopularity of William, the death of the sole surviving son of the Princess Anne, and the internecine fury of the struggle between the two Houses of Convocation, the two Houses of Parliament, and the two parties in the House of Commons, made a Jacobite restoration probable. It appeared in 1701 when the Tories, being the ascendant party in the country and the House, attacked William and his Whig supporters with a ferocity that presaged civil war. The occasion was an Irish one—the report of the commissioners on the forfeited Irish estates, showing that grossly extravagant grants had been made to the King's Dutch favourites. While the Tory majority in the Commons insisted upon the resumption of these grants, the Whig majority in the Lords held out against the Bill, till civil war seemed almost in sight. However, not the Lords only, but William bowed before the storm. The Resumption Bill was passed, the King's friends were dismissed from office, and a Tory Ministry installed in their stead. These concessions, however, were so far from conciliating the party in the House and country which had extorted them that the result of a new election was a Parliament more decidedly and violently Tory than its predecessor. Not content with the resumption of the Irish estates, with the dismissal of the Whig Ministry and its replacement by a Tory administration, the victors pressed for the destruction of their defeated foes. They proceeded to impeach William's wisest counsellor—the late Lord Chancellor, Somers—his dearest friend—the Earl of Portland—the Earl of Oxford, the stanchest of the Whigs, and their ablest financier, Lord Halifax. Again the House of Lords made a stand, this time a dogged stand, and only the temporary expedient of a prorogation averted a collision.

During the prorogation Swift's pamphlet appeared to counsel moderation of party spirit, to deprecate servile party allegiance, and above all, to denounce *dominatio plebis*, the tyranny of a party, as at least as oppressive and mischievous as the tyranny of a despot. Swift's detractors, who are at such pains to point out that this pamphlet was written in defence, if not of the Whig platform, at least of the Whig party, forget to add that it was written when the prospects of that party were hopeless. What brought him into this sinking galley, when he might just as well then, as later, have been taken as pilot aboard the boat that triumphed? As a matter of fact, this pamphlet, which is the main basis of the charge of political apostacy brought against Swift, is a demonstrative vindication of his disinterestedness. When it was written only a prophet could have foreseen what only a miracle apparently could have produced—the sudden and sweeping revulsion of feeling in favour of the Whigs which swept over England like the wave that follows an earthquake. A king's folly is naturally and fortunately proportioned to his power, since the higher he is up, the more he is out of hearing, sight and touch of the people, and the more likely he is to make fatal mistakes; and few kings for this reason have made graver blunders of this unsympathetic sort than *Le Grand Monarque*. Again and again he played into the hands of his deadliest enemy, William, but never more completely and opportunely than when, on the death of James II. at St. Germain, he recognized the Pretender as King of England. The effect in England of this fatuous recognition was revolutionary. Instantaneously it steadied William's tottering throne, and reversing as with an engine lever the set of political feeling, made the Tories seem the traitors deserving of impeachment, and the Whigs the patriot preservers of their country. The death of James II. and Louis' recognition of the Pretender occurred in September 1701, and in the following November a general election put the Whigs by an overwhelming majority in power. During their brief reign Swift was flattered by the intimacy and by the promises of preferment of their leaders, Somers, Sunderland and Halifax, but William was not long in following James to the grave, and the accession of Anne meant the return to power of the Tories.

Anne, so far as she was anything at all intellectually, was a Churchwoman of a high and narrow type. Theology is the sole science women effect, and the less intelligent the woman the more profound invariably is her conversance with this mystery. Anne accordingly was a profound theologian, and her narrow High-Church theology bound her to the Tories by conviction; but by her infatuated affection for the Duchess of Marlborough she was insensibly and insidiously drawn towards the Whigs. The Duke was all things to all Princes that he might betray all; and he adopted Anne's prejudices, as he had adopted the cause of James, and as he had adopted the cause of William only till it became more to his advantage to renounce each. He was almost as detached from English parties as William, and for William's reason—that his hopes and interests lay abroad and in the war, where he won glory, rank and what he valued more than either—more than all—wealth. As, therefore, the Whig party was the war party, Marlborough was at heart a Whig. "I resolved," said his Duchess, "from the very beginning of the Queen's reign to try whether I could not by degrees make impressions on her mind more favourable to the Whigs." It was because of, and not in spite of, this resolve that she and the Duke feigned Toryism at first to make their footing firm. "As soon as Anne was seated on the throne," says the Duchess, "the Tories whom she usually called by the agreeable name of the Church-party, became the distinguished objects of royal favour. . . . I am firmly persuaded that, notwithstanding her extraordinary affection for me, and the entire devotion which my Lord Marlborough and my Lord Godolphin had for many years shown to her service, they would not have had so great a share of her favour and confidence, if they had not been reckoned in the number of the Tories." It is odd to think that this dull Queen and "the greatest genius of his age," Swift, should have had the same precise political views, and should have stood in the same precise relation to the Whigs. To Swift, also, the Tories meant "the Church-party," and the Whigs were acceptable only so long as in Church matters they were Tory. As it was some time before the Whig leaders dared risk the forfeiture of the Queen's countenance by showing themselves the reverse of Tory in Church matters, it was some time also before Swift broke with them; but when he did break with them, be it remembered, they were in power. The pamphlet, "On the Dissensions at Athens and Rome," which won him the favour of these leaders, was published when their prospects were desperate; the pamphlets, "The Sentiments of a Church of England Man," and the still more vehement and brilliant onslaught on the toleration policy of the Whigs—the Letter in support of the Test—which cost him the favour of these leaders, were published when they were in power. It took, however, some years and some of Marlborough's most brilliant victories to put the Whigs in power, and meanwhile the Tories were pressing the advantage which the accession of a High-Church Queen gave them, to attempt the virtual reversal of the Toleration Act of 1689. The Bill "To Prevent Occasional Conformity," which was carried by immense majorities in the House of Commons, subjected not holders of office only, but all electors for boroughs also, to the provisions of the Test Act. To enter a dissenting place of worship, after having once taken the sacrament according to the rite of the Church of England, was a crime to be punished, on the first offence, by a heavy fine, on the second, by transportation. As to receive the sacrament according to the Church of England rite was to be an indispensable qualification, not for office only, but for the franchise, it will be admitted that the measure was sufficiently reactionary to justify the storm it aroused. As not all the influence of the Court could induce the Lords to pass the Bill, it was reintroduced in the following session into the Commons, promptly passed there by an overwhelming majority, and as promptly, though not as decisively, rejected by the Lords. "I wish," writes Swift, upon this rejection, "you had been here for ten days during the highest and warmest reign of party and faction that I ever knew or read of, upon the Bill against Occasional Conformity, which two days ago was, upon the first reading, rejected by the Lords. It was so universal that I observed the dogs in the streets much more contumelious and quarrelsome than usual; and the very night before the Bill went up, a committee of Whig and Tory cats had a very warm and loud debate upon the roof of our house. But why should we wonder at that, when the very ladies are split asunder into high-church and low, and out of zeal for religion, have hardly time to say their prayers."

Marlborough used all his influence to counteract in the Lords his own disingenuous vote in favour of the Bill; but this influence was slight compared with that which he wielded when the Bill was reintroduced in the following session. In the interval, Blenheim had been fought and won, and Marlborough's victory in the field was not more decisive than the political victory it won for him at home. Intoxicated with so brilliant a British triumph, England became of Marlborough's party, whichever that might be, and so made him strong enough to show his true Whig colours. Even the Tory majority in the Commons contributed to his triumph by the folly with which it rushed to its own destruction. In spite of the defection of its foremost champion, St. John, and of the now open opposition of the Ministry, it passed again the Bill against Occasional Conformity, and, in order to force it through the Lords, designed to tack it to a Money Bill, to the disgust and alienation of the more moderate of its own side. This petulant attempt to wreck the constitution—to pull down the house if they were not allowed to be the master—helped to swell the Whig majority which was returned at the ensuing election, and which, with the help of the victory of Ramillies, kept the Whigs in power for over five years. During these years they passed Swift over again and again for preferment, while persistently turning a deaf ear to his reiterated application for the restoration to the Irish Church of the Irish First-fruits and Tenths, which had been remitted in England by Anne for the augmentation of small livings. This small boon—it meant but a little over £1,000 a year to the Irish Church—was promised at last on the condition that Swift would consent to the repeal of the Test Act in Ireland—a safe offer to the man who had written the *Letter on the Sacramental Test.*

It may be said—indeed it cannot be gainsaid—that the writer of this brilliant and biting plea for the political extinction of dissenters, was sanguine to hope for favours from a party whose backbone was dissent. For my own part, I admit that nothing more astonishes me than Swift's astonishment at the offence *A Tale of a Tub* gave to Christians, and the *Letter on the Sacramental Test* gave to Whigs. But Swift was one of those egotists who can never get far enough

E

away from themselves to see how they look to others, He knew at least this, however, that the fiercest of the fierce fights between Whig and Tory had raged for years about this one question—the political disabilities of dissenters—and that nothing more distinctively or effectively Tory upon this question than his *Letter on the Sacramental Test* had appeared in all these years. It was published when the Whigs were at the culminating point of their power, as the Whig pamphlet, *On the Dissentions at Athens and Rome*, was published when the party was at the apogee of power, yet Swift is charged with interested political apostacy! As a matter of fact, in that age of frenzied political gambling, Swift was one of the few leaders on either side who never counted the cost of declaring uncompromising and unpalatable principles. That he resented the bill when it came to be paid, I admit. He was enraged at the Whig neglect of himself and of his suit for his Church, and he welcomed the chance of revenge—far more than he welcomed the chance of promotion—which the turn of the wheel in the favour of the Tories gave him. He was a good hater; to smite the enemy hip and thigh was more to him than to fly upon the spoil; and that pompous political prig, Godolphin, miscalculated not his time only, but his man, when he ventured to befool Swift about the First-fruits affair at the critical moment of his Ministry's fortunes. Godolphin's foolishness, indeed, cost his party more than the defection of Swift, since it was he who insisted upon the prosecution of Dr. Sacheverell because the incriminated sermon reflected upon himself. "The impeachment of Dr. Sacheverell," writes Swift, "arose from a foolish, passionate pique of the Earl of Godolphin, whom this divine was supposed in a sermon to have reflected on, under the name of 'Volpone,' as my Lord Somers, a few months after confessed to me; and, at the same time, that he had earnestly and in vain endeavoured to dissuade the Earl from that attempt." I cannot help thinking that too much stress has been laid upon this Sacheverell impeachment —on the one side, by Lord Campbell, who thought that but for it the Whigs "would have continued undisturbed in office till their tenure had been confirmed by the accession of the House of Hanover," and, on the other side, by Edmund Burke, who held that the prosecution was instituted to secure a clear, authentic and recorded declaration of the principles on which the Revolution was founded. In fact, the condemnation of this foolish sermon of a mountebank preacher was rather the occasion, than the cause of the fall of the Whigs—a mere rag, so to say, picked up in the street, soiled and flimsy, but of the proper colour, and used, therefore, as a flag needed by an army advancing already to the attack. It happened at the moment when the country was sick of the Whigs, and the Queen of the Marlboroughs, whom Harley, by the help of Mrs. Masham, had succeeded in undermining. The helpless Queen, having now lost her husband, who, however feeble and foolish, was her sole disinterested friend, and having at last escaped from the insolent control of the Duchess of Marlborough, was, like a hermit-crab, glad of the shelter of a new shell, which she found in Harley's creature, Mrs. Masham. Harley, having thus secured the Queen, proceeded to make good his hold on the country by successful overtures to Swift at the moment of his exasperation with Godolphin —a happy moment for the Tories. While Swift's *Examiner* won and kept the country to their side, his personal influence held in harness together their two incongruously-yoked leaders, Harley and St. John, so long as their co-operation was possible. But when the inevitable split came, the end came. A violent rupture between Harley and St. John (now Lords Oxford and Bolingbroke) in the Queen's presence whose immediate result was the dismissal of Oxford, hastened Anne's death, which, five days later, involved Bolingbroke and his party in the ruin of his rival.

During the four years they held office they did Ireland one supreme service by the appointment of Swift to the Deanery of St. Patrick's—a fulcrum for the lever wherewith he moved our country on the course she has followed to her advantage to this day. For the rest, what can be said for their government, or for those which immediately preceded it, or for Walpole's long and foul reign of cancerous corruption which followed it? Admirers of the British Constitution had better not look into the characters and credentials of its fathers, unless on the principle which was the secret of the conversion of the Jew, Abraham, in the second story of Boccaccio. Certainly no one can look down the filthy backstairs of one and all of these governments without recalling Burke's description of statecraft:—"The very name of a politician and statesman is sure to cause terror and hatred. It has always connected with it the ideas of treachery, cruelty, fraud and tyranny; and those writers who have unveiled the mysteries of State-Freemasonry have ever been held in general detestation for even knowing so perfectly a theory so detestable."

In truth, no statesman of his time and of his rank was more consistent and disinterested than Swift, and only those who hold a political party to be as integral, infallible and unchanging as a church—*quod semper, quod ubique, quod ab omnibus*—can charge him plausibly with political apostacy.

CHAPTER V.

IN POWER.

WIFT'S early leanings and writings, then, were on the side of the political party with which he waged such bitter war all his later life; but that he sold his principles for promotion in the Church, or for power in the State can seem probable only to those who have not been at the trouble to ascertain his principles—those of an Irish Tory. The highest Tory in Ireland, as he told King William, would make a tolerable Whig in England; because in Ireland the Stuart cause was the cause of the Catholics, and the more a man was an adherent of the Church of England, so much the more was he an adherent of the Revolution. Now of Swift it might almost be said that he was a Church of England man and nothing else. While he scorns the Irish Catholic, he hates the Irish Presbyterian. He can afford to hate him he argues, since the impotence of the Irish Catholic renders the Church of England independent of a

Protestant alliance with the Presbyterian. "It is agreed among naturalists," he writes, "that a lion"—the Irish Catholics—"is a larger, a stronger, and more dangerous enemy than a cat"—the Irish Presbyterians—"yet if a man were to have his choice, either a lion at his foot fast bound with three or four chains, his teeth drawn out, and his claws pared to the quick, or an angry cat in full liberty at his throat, he would take no long time to determine."

So far as the State was concerned, then, Swift was a Whig, an adherent of the Revolution, and of all the political principles of the Revolution; but in everything that concerned the Church he was an extreme Tory. When the Revolution and its principles had taken ineradicable hold and Jacobitism had become little more than a drunken toast, Swift had only his Church to fear for; and for it he had to fear only the liberalizing tendencies—in such shapes as the Repeal or the Relaxation of the Test Act—of the Whigs. It was not then, in his own interests, but in the interests of his Church that Swift deserted the Whigs, and he deserted them, moreover, when it was to his own interests to adhere to them as the party in power and at the height of their power.

When, however, Swift first joined the Whigs as a political recruit under the shifty Sunderland, the ship was sinking. He had arranged to resign his living to devote himself to this service, when, even before the resignation was completed, Sunderland fell, "and I," writes Swift to his successor in Kilroot, "fell with him." It was not the last of Swift's disappointments. "I remember," he writes years after to Lord Bolingbroke, "when I was a little boy, I felt a great fish at the end of my line, which I drew up almost on the ground, but it dropped in, and the disappointment vexes me to this day, and I believe it was the type of all my future disappointments." He did not, however, repent or retract the proposed resignation, but settled down for the present at Moor Park, and there wrote the *Battle of the Books* and revised the already written *Tale of a Tub*. May I say again in passing, that even more astonishing than the genius shown in a *Tale of a Tub* is Swift's astonishment at the offence it gave, not to Catholics and Presbyterians alone, but to members of his own Church. No man, it seems to me, could unconsciously run such amuck against Christianity, and be quite sane; yet Swift was really confounded that Christians were scandalised by the scurrilous and indiscriminating ferocity of the satire. How the man who wrote it could remain a minister or member of any Christian Church perplexes the reader; but Swift was perplexed that it barred his way to a bishopric.

Hardly had Swift completed this literary work when Sir William Temple's death threw him alone upon the world, with only a Prince's promise to trust to for his future. Having first vainly endeavoured to remind King William—through a debauched and discredited favourite—of his promise to him of a prebend—he tried to recall himself to that Prince's memory by dedicating to him the first volume of *Temple's Remains*. Failing here also, he fell back upon an appointment as chaplain and secretary to Lord Berkeley, who was setting out to Ireland as one of its three Lord Justices. The post of chaplain he had accepted only as a mere and honorary addition to the secretaryship; yet on his arrival in Dublin he was intrigued out of the secretaryship by a man named Bush, and Swift was fain to content himself with the chaplaincy and Lord Berkeley's promise of the first Irish preferment that happened to fall vacant. But not even in this was faith kept with him. When the wealthiest Deanery in Ireland—that of Derry—did fall vacant it was put up by Bush to auction, and knocked down to Dr. Theophilus Bolton for the bribe of a thousand guineas, which Swift was neither able nor willing to offer. That this was not an exceptional instance of the manner in which that Church Swift so venerated was officered, may be inferred from his own delightful description of how its dignitaries came to discredit it. "Excellent and moral men have been selected on every occasion of a vacancy by the English Prime Minister. But it unfortunately has uniformly happened that as these worthy divines crossed Hounslow Heath on their way to Ireland to take possession of their bishoprics, they have been regularly robbed and murdered by the highwaymen frequenting that common, who seized upon their robes and patents, came over to Ireland, and are consequently bishops in their stead."

Swift was in some degree indemnified for his disappointment of the Deanery of Derry by his presentation to the livings of Laracor, Agher, and Rathbeggan, worth together something over £200 a year, and a little later by the gift of the Prebend of Dulavin in St. Patrick's, which made some small addition to this income. He had hardly been instituted into these preferments before he quitted them and Ireland for England and politics; for the triumph of the Tories involved the recall of Lord Berkeley and his brother Lord Justices, who were superseded by the Earl of Rochester. It was the lack of all moderation in this triumph of the Tories in the House of Commons which produced, as I have shown, Swift's first political pamphlet—*Discourse on the Dissensions in Athens and Rome*—an attack upon what he called *Dominatio Plebis*, upon the tyranny and factiousness of the House of Commons, and upon the danger to the Constitution of the consequent disturbance of its balance. Compared with Swift's other political writings this pamphlet is fanciful, affected and pedantic—wheeling round above its mark rather than swooping down upon it; but it is vigorously written, pertinent, and above all opportune. Unless you keep in mind that opportuneness is everything in a political pamphlet you will be at a loss to understand the effect of this tract upon the public and upon Swift's political fortunes. The secret of the success of the popular orator as expressed in that happy image:—"The orator rolls back upon his audience in a torrent what he received from them in a mist"—is the secret also of the success of the political pamphlet; and Swift happened to hit the taste and the feeling and even the event of the moment—for Louis XIV.'s recognition of the Pretender on the death of James II., was an object lesson to the English people of where such "Dissensions" might land them.

Swift now was caressed, flattered and promised great things by the Whig chiefs, only to be disappointed utterly and at all points when they came into power. They promoted neither himself nor his mission from his Church about the restoration to it of the First-fruits; while what seemed to him the very bulwark of his Church—the Test

Act—was in imminent danger of being repealed by them. Hence Swift's alienation from the Whigs. They befooled him about the First-fruits, and alarmed him by the appointment of a Presbyterian Viceroy with a probable view to the repeal of the Test Act, while they more than once passed him over for promotion. In truth, they found that he was not a hearty Whig, or a Whig at all in anything except his Irish-Protestant adhesion to the Revolution. His *Sentiments of a Church of England Man*, in which Whig principles of toleration were controverted generally, and his pamphlet in the form of a letter from an Irish to an English Member of Parliament, in which the special application of these principles to the repeal of the Test Act was denounced with surprising force, spirit and humour, showed the Whig chiefs that in all but his anti-Jacobitism, he was a Tory of the Tories. If he had written to advocate the principles and the policy he denounced, or even if he had not written at all on the subject, the Whig chiefs would have kept faith with him as regards both his own promotion and the promotion of the mission his Church had entrusted to him. As it is, it seems to me, they as little deserved Swift's charge against them of ingratitude, as Swift deserved their charge against him of apostacy. If Swift's principles were on sale, he would certainly have got more for them from the Whigs than he afterwards got from the Tories; but he never sold his principles, nor even changed them; and he retired to sulk in his tent when, if he had fought heartily for the Whigs, he must have commanded a bishopric.

Swift remained sulking in his tent till the prosecution of Sacheverell let out the gathering discontent of the country and the court, and swept the Whigs from power. Upon the Tories coming in he was again commissioned by the Irish bishops to appeal to the Government for the restoration of the First-fruits and Tenths to the Irish Church. Upon reaching London he was, he says, clutched at by the drowning Whigs, whom, however, he shook roughly off, and got introduced to Harley "as a discontented person, who was ill-used for not being Whig enough." Harley, whose single but singular gift was discernment of men, clutched at Swift even more eagerly than the drowning Whigs, since, as he afterwards confessed, of all the Whig writers he feared only Swift, and was resolved to have him. He undertook to carry through speedily and successfully the First-fruits affair—which he did— while Swift repaid him by his masterly conduct of the Tory organ, *The Examiner.* The style of Swift's "Examiners" is perfect of its kind and for its purpose. His own rather bald definition of a good style—"proper words in proper places"—expresses the form of these papers precisely, while their matter, like the lead of a bullet, is calculated nicely, and only to serve a single object—to go straight and strong and true to its mark. The admiration Swift's political tracts excites is of the kind excited by a steam-engine —admiration of power, precision, and such exquisite adaptation of means to a single end that there is neither waste nor want, friction nor dispersion.

But the masterly advocacy of the Tory policy of peace in *The Examiner* was not the sole or the chief service Swift did the Administration. He was admitted to the "Saturday Dinners," a kind of inner Cabinet, consisting of Harley, Harcourt and St. John, and he helped both to form and to formulate the policy of the Ministry at home and abroad. In fact, he reached at a bound such a pinnacle of power as might well have turned any man's head, and which did, perhaps, turn his. The sole evidence of this we have, however, is that of an unfriendly witness, Bishop Kennett, who notes in his diary for 1713 the swagger of Swift at the height of his power:—" Swift came into the coffee-house and had a bow from everybody but me. When I came to the antechamber before prayers, Dr. Swift was the principal man of talk and business, and acted as minister of requests. He was soliciting the Earl of Arran to speak to his brother, the Duke of

Ormond, to get a chaplain's place established in the garrison of Hull, for Mr. Fiddes, a clergyman in that neighbourhood, who had lately been in jail, and published sermons to pay fees. He was promising Mr. Thorold to undertake with my Lord Treasurer that according to his petition he should obtain a salary of £200 per annum, as minister of the English Church at Rotterdam. He stopped F. Gwynne, Esq., going in with the red bag to the Queen, and told him aloud he had something to say to him from my Lord Treasurer. He talked with the son of Dr. Davenant to be sent abroad, and took out his pocket-book and wrote down several things as memoranda to do for him. He turned to the fire, and took out his gold watch, and telling him the time of day, complained it was very late. A gentleman said 'it was too fast.' 'How can I help it,' says the Doctor, 'if the courtiers give me a watch that won't go right?' Then he instructed a young nobleman that the best poet in England was Mr. Pope (a Papist) who had begun a translation of Homer into English verse, for which, he said, he must have them all subscribe. 'For,' says he, 'the author *shall* not begin to print till I have a thousand guineas for him.' Lord Treasurer, after leaving the Queen, came through the room, beckoning Dr. Swift to follow him; both went off just before prayers."

This is prejudiced evidence, little likely to minimise Swift's swagger or to magnify his influence, or the beneficence and disinterestedness of his use of it. He coined every penny of this influence for the enrichment and the advancement of friends and *protégés*. No doubt he loved power, and loved even the parade of power, but these are not singular weaknesses even in a man of such commanding intellect; whereas he was more than singular in the truth and strength of his friendships. His most prejudiced enemy cannot but be struck by the contrast between the zeal with which in these days of his power he urged the claims of his Church and of his friends, and the slackness of his pursuit of preferment for himself. He did not press for it; he hardly expected it; while he wished for it almost less for its own sake, than for the sake of saving his pride the appearance of failure. In his *Journal to Stella*, wherein, remember, he writes as a man speaking aloud to himself, he says, "I never got a penny from them, nor expect it. . . . Remember, if I am used ill and ungratefully, as I have formerly been, 'tis what I am prepared for, and shall not wonder at it. Yet I am now envied and thought in high favour, and have every day numbers of considerable men teasing me to solicit for them. And the ministry all use me perfectly well, and all that know them say they love me. Yet I count upon nothing, nor will but upon your love and kindness. They think me useful; they pretended they were afraid of none but me; and that they resolved to have me; they have often confessed this; yet all this makes little impression on me.... To return without some mark of distinction would look extremely little, and I would likewise gladly be somewhat richer than I am." Nor, when the promotion which was to be his at last—the Deanery of St. Patrick's—was dangled before him, did he show undue or undignified eagerness to snatch at it. This preferment was in the gift of the Duke of Ormond, who disliked the present Dean, Sterne, so much that he objected to his promotion to a bishopric, which was necessary in order to create a vacancy for Swift. That Swift did not take particular pains to overcome this objection of the Duke's may be inferred from his own account of the matter to Stella. " I went to-day, by appointment, to the cock-pit to talk with the Duke of Ormond. He repeated the same proposals of any other deanery, &c. ... I desired he would put me out of the case and do as he pleased. Then with great kindness he said he would consent; but would do it for no man alive but me, &c." Compare the zeal with which Swift pressed the suits of others with his haughty reluctance to be importunate for his own promotion, and you will see that his pride was of nobler stuff than Bishop Kennett's account of its vulgar parade would suggest. But there is even better evidence of this, and also of the disinterested loyalty of Swift's friendships, in his adhesion to Harley in his fall. "I have been asked," he writes, "to join with those people now in power, but I will not do it. I told Lord Oxford I would go with him when he was out, and now he begs it of me and I cannot refuse him. I meddle not with his faults, as he was a Minister of State; but you know his personal kindness to me was excessive; he distinguished and chose me above all other men, while he was great, and his letter to me the other day was the most moving imaginable."

But even while Swift wrote, Queen Anne was breathing her last, and her death meant the political extinction not alone of "those people now in power," but of the entire Tory party, of Swift's hopes and of all his prospects of promotion.

The political power which the Tory chiefs lost irrecoverably was at the mercy of a hundred accidents, from that of a prince's fancy or favour to that of his death; whereas Swift's political power was independent of the life or of the favour of princes, parliaments, ministries or people. And in thus contrasting the relative positions and powers of Swift, and of his sovereigns and their ministers—in marking how he towered above them intrinsically as much as to the world's eye he ranked below them—it is well to remember that this contrast was an ever-present thought and root of bitterness in Swift's own mind. I suppose no man with anything like Swift's powers of observation had ever anything like his opportunities of observing the little wisdom wherewith the world is governed. He had daily for years measured himself against the men who guided the destinies of England directly, and indirectly those of Europe, and he found and he felt that in all but the little and low arts of the politician he towered above them. And these backstairs and chambermaid arts of the politician intensified the bitterness of his scorn. In a memorandum in Swift's handwriting, found among his papers, he compares politicians with pickpockets, and declares that the qualities needed for success in each profession are precisely the same, adding, "I have personally known more than half a dozen—in their hour esteemed equally—to excel in both."

Such were the ideas of the mental and moral calibre of English statesmanship which Swift took with him into his Irish exile, where its intolerable effects met and moved him at every turn to fell rage. No man had a deeper natural horror of oppression and of injustice, and nowhere did helpless oppression and injustice make a more piteous appeal.

CHAPTER VI.

THE IRELAND OF SWIFT'S DAY.

AN unprejudiced picture of Ireland as it appeared and appealed to Swift in his exile will properly preface an account of his work there. It alone could adequately explain his "fell rage," justify the measures to which it moved him, and account for their success. In this chapter, therefore, I shall present my readers with two pictures of the Ireland of Swift's day, taken from unimpeachable sources,—from the weightiest organ of that English party, the Tory, which has ever been least in sympathy with Irish suffering—the *Quarterly Review;* and from a statement of the Irish case made to Walpole by Swift, under a sense that every word of it would be checked, and if possible challenged, by

Walpole's own creatures—the agents of the misgovernment it impeached.

English writers with an admirable magnanimity confess the faults of their fathers. It is true they can afford to confess them since only their fathers are ever in fault; while nothing makes a Pharisee feel so holy as his full and frank confession of a Publican's sins. I have myself read pages of Macaulay which have moved me in the same way and in the same degree as the triumphant recital by a Salvation Army convert of all the abandoned infamies of his past. The *Quarterly* also in its picture of the Ireland of Swift's day, wears the white sheet of vicarious repentance with an almost ostentatious grace.

"Even now," it says, "on recalling these cruel statutes, which completed between 1665 and 1699 the annihilation of Irish trade, it is impossible not to feel something of the indignation which burned in Swift. In 1660 there was every prospect that in a few years Ireland might become a happy and prosperous country. Her natural advantages were great. In no regions within the compass of the British Isles was the soil more fertile. As pasture land she was to the modern world what Argos was to the ancient. She was not without navigable rivers; the ports and harbours with which Nature had bountifully provided her were the envy of every maritime nation in Europe; and her geographical position was eminently propitious to commercial enterprise. For the first time in her history she was at peace. The aborigines had at last succumbed to the Englishry. A race of sturdy and industrious colonists were rapidly changing the face of the country. Agriculture was thriving. A remunerative trade in live cattle and in miscellaneous farm produce had been opened with England; a still more remunerative trade in manufactured wool was holding out prospects still more promising. There were even hopes of an extensive mercantile connection with the colonies. But the dawn of this fair day was soon overcast. Impelled partly by jealousy and partly by that short-sighted selfishness which was, in former days, so unhappily conspicuous in her commercial relations with subject states, England proceeded to the systematic destruction of Irish commerce and of Irish industrial art. First came the two statutes forbidding the importation of live cattle and farm produce into England, and Ireland was a once deprived of her chief source of revenue. Then came the statutes which annihilated her colonial trade. Crushing and terrible though these blows were, she still, however, continued to struggle on, crippled and dispirited, indeed, but not entirely without heart. But in 1699 was enacted the statute which completed her ruin. By this she was prevented from seeking any vent for her raw and manufactured wool, except in England and Wales, where the duties imposed on both these commodities were so heavy as virtually to exclude them from the market. The immediate result of this atrocious measure was to turn flourishing villages into deserts, and to throw between twenty and thirty thousand able-bodied and industrious artizans on public charity. The ultimate result of all these measures was the complete paralysis of operative energy, the emigration of the only class who were of benefit to the community, and the commencement of a period of unprecedented wretchedness and degradation. The condition of Ireland between 1700 and 1750 was in truth such as no historian, who was not prepared to have his narrative laid aside with disgust and incredulity, would venture to depict. If analogy is to be sought for it, it must be sought in the scenes through which, in the frightful fiction of Monti, the disembodied spirit of Bassville was condemned to roam. In a time of peace the unhappy island suffered all the most terrible calamities which follow in the train of war. Famine succeeding famine decimated the provincial villages, and depopulated whole regions.

"Travellers have described how their way has lain through districts strewn like a battle-field with unburied corpses, which lay some in ditches, some on the roadside, and some on heaps of offal, the prey of dogs and carrion birds. Even when there was no actual famine, the food of the rustic vulgar was often such as our domestic animals would reject with disgust. Their ordinary fare was buttermilk and potatoes, and, when these failed, they were at the mercy of fortune. Frequently the pot of the wretched cottier contained nothing but the product of the marsh and the waste-ground. The flesh of a horse which had died in harness, the flesh of sylvan vermin, even when corruption had begun to do its revolting work, were devoured voraciously. Burdy tells us that these famishing savages would surreptitiously bleed the cattle which they had not the courage to steal, and boiling the blood with sorrel, would convert the sickening mixture into food. Epidemic diseases and all the loathsome maladies which were the natural inheritance of men whose food was the food of hogs and jackals, whose dwellings were scarcely distinguishable from dung-hills, and whose personal habits were filthy even to beastliness, raged with a fury rarely witnessed in western latitudes. Not less deplorable was the spectacle presented by the country itself. "Whoever took a journey through Ireland," says Swift, 'would be apt to imagine himself travelling in Lapland or Iceland." In the south, in the east, and in the west, stretched vast tracts of land untilled and unpeopled, mere waste and solitude."

How insane would such a description by an Englishman of English misgovernment sound to the English contemporaries of Swift! It seems a pity—for Ireland—that light should travel so slowly to English eyes that they can see things as they are to-day in Ireland only a century hence. Nor do they always perceive that in the Ireland of a century since (which alone they can clearly see) lie the roots of the Ireland of to-day. Take, for instance, the landlord and tenant quarrel, which any writer in to-day's *Quarterly* would think adequately explained by the epigram, "Tenant right is landlord wrong." Yet to-day's *Quarterly* can give the following description of the relations of landlord and tenant in Swift's day without a misgiving that he is grubbing among the roots of the upas tree.

"The principal landlords resided in England, leaving as their lieutenants a class of men known in Irish history as middlemen. It may be doubted whether since the days of the Roman Publicani oppression and rapacity had ever assumed a shape so odious as they assumed in these men. The middleman was, as a rule, entirely destitute of education; his tastes were low, his habits debauched and recklessly extravagant. Long familiarity with such scenes as we have described had rendered him not merely indifferent to human sufferings but ruthless and brutal.

All the tenancies held under him were at rack-rent, and with the extraction of that rent, or what was, in kind, equivalent to that rent, began and ended his relations with the tenants. As many of these tenants were impecunious serfs, often insolvent, and always in arrears, it was only by keeping a wary eye upon their movements, and by pouncing with seasonable avidity on anything of which they might happen to become possessed, either by the labour of their hands, or by some accident of fortune, that he could turn them to account. Sometimes the produce of the potato-plot became his prey, sometimes their agricultural tools; not unfrequently he would seize everything which belonged to them, and driving them with their wives and children, often under circumstances of revolting cruelty, out of their cabins, send them to perish of cold and hunger in the open country. Nor were the Irish provincial gentry in any way superior to the middle men. Swift, indeed, regarded them with still greater detestation. As public men, they were chiefly remarkable for their savage oppression of the clergy, for the mercilessness with which they exacted their rack-rents from the tenantry, and for the mean ingenuity with which they contrived to make capital out of the miseries of their country. In private life they were dissolute, litigious, and arrogant, and their vices would comprehend some of the worst vices incident to man — inhuman cruelty, tyranny in its most repulsive aspects, brutal appetites forcibly gratified, or gratified under circumstances scarcely less atrocious, and an ostentatious lawlessness which revelled unchecked either by civil authority or by religion."

The picture would be incomplete without an account of the efforts of Church and State to remedy all this wrong and robbery.

"We have already alluded to the statutes which annihilated the trade and prostrated the industrial energy of the country. Equally iniquitous and oppressive was the alienation of revenue. On that revenue had been quartered the parasites and mistresses of succeeding generations of English kings. Almost all the most remunerative public posts were sinecures in the possession of men who resided in England. Indeed, some of these sinecurists had never set foot on Irish earth. But nothing was more derogatory to England than the scandalous condition of the Protestant hierarchy. On that body depended not only the spiritual welfare, but the education of the multitude, and their responsibility was the greater in consequence of the inhibitions which had been laid by the Legislature on the Catholic priesthood. But the Protestant clergy were, as a class, a scandal to Christendom. Many of the bishops would have disgraced the hierarchy of Henry III. Their ignorance, their apathy, their nepotism, their sensuality, passed into proverbs.

It was not uncommon for them to abandon even the semblance of their sacred character, and to live the life of jovial country squires, their palaces ringing with revelry, their dioceses with anarchy. If their sees were not to their taste, they resided elsewhere. The Bishop of Down, for example, resided at Hammersmith, where he lived for twenty years without having once during the whole of that time set foot in his diocese. That there were a few noble exceptions must in justice be admitted. No Churchman could pronounce the names of Berkeley, King and Synge, without reverence. But the virtues of these illustrious prelates had little influence either on their degenerate peers or on the inferior clergy. Of this body it would not be too much to say that no section of the demoralized society, of which they formed a part, were more demoralized or so completely despicable."

I hope the moral weight of this Tory testimony will be held to counterbalance the elephantine weight of the style in which it is couched. Queen's evidence need not be expressed in Queen's English to be of value And such an unimpeachable description of the country as it appeared and appealed to Swift is of indispensable value to those who wish to understand the motives, means, objects and results of his Irish crusade. Swift's own statement of the Irish case to Walpole, which I shall now proceed to give, is of so much less value as it covers so much less of the ground. Southey somewhere says that letters often tell more of the character of the man they are addressed to, than of the character of the writer; and Swift of all men was least likely to take his eye for a moment off the person he was addressing. His letter to Walpole, then, was an *argumentum ad hominem*, a bald recital of such facts and arguments only as would appeal to that sordid cynic, whose single principle of government was that of the "Unjust Steward." Since this Minister regarded Ireland as a Japanese host regards the live fish from which he cuts slices with a deft avoidance of a vital part, Swift aimed chiefly to convince Walpole that he was cutting too much and too deeply if he wished the creature to live a little longer.

"The first and greatest shock our trade received," he writes in this state paper, "was from an Act passed in the reign of King William, in the Parliament of England, prohibiting the exportation of wool manufactured in Ireland; an Act, as the event plainly shows, fuller of greediness than good policy; an Act as beneficial to France and Spain as it has been destructive to Ireland. At the passing of this fatal Act, the condition of our trade was glorious and flourishing, though in no way interfering with the English. We made no broad-cloths above 6s. per yard; coarse druggets, bays shalloons, worsted damasks, strong draught-works, slight half-works, and gaudy stuffs, were the only products of our looms. These were partly consumed by the meanest of our people, and partly sent to the northern nations, from whom we had in exchange timber, hemp, flax, pitch, tar, and hard dollars. At the time the current money of Ireland was foreign silver, a man could hardly receive £100, without finding the coin of all the northern powers, and of every prince of the empire among it. This money was returned into England for fine cloths, silks, etc., for our own wear, for rent, for coals, for hardware, and all other English manufactures, and in a great measure supplied the London merchants with foreign silver for exportation. The repeated clamours of the English weavers produced this Act, so destructive to themselves and us. They looked with envious eyes upon our prosperity, and complained of being undersold by us in those commodities which they themselves did not deal in. At their instances the Act was passed, and we lost our profitable northern trade. Have they got it? No; surely you have found out they have ever since declined in the trade they so happily possessed? You shall find (if I am rightly informed) towns without one loom in them which entirely subsisted upon the woollen manufactory before the passing of this unhappy Bill;

and I will try, if I can, to give the true reason for the decay of their trade and our calamities. Three parts in four of that district of the town where I dwell were English manufacturers, whom either misfortunes in trade, little petty debts contracted through idleness, or the pressures of numerous families, had driven into our cheap country. These were employed in working up our coarse wool, while the finest was sent to England. Several of these had taken children of the native Irish apprentices to them, who, being humbled by the forfeiture of upwards of three millions by the Revolution, were obliged to stoop to mechanic industry. Upon the passing of this Bill we were obliged to dismiss thousands of these people from our service. Those who had settled their affairs returned home and over-stocked England with workmen. Those whose debts were unsatisfied went to France, Spain, the Netherlands, where they met with good encouragement, whereby the natives of these countries, having got a firm footing in the trade, being acute fellows, soon became as good workmen as any we have, and supply the foreign manufactories with a constant recruit of artizans—our Island lying much more under pasture than any in Europe. The foreigners (notwithstanding all the restrictions the English parliament has bound us up with) are furnished with the greatest quantity of our choicest wool. I need not tell you, sir, that a custom-house oath is held as little sacred here as in England; or that it is common for masters of vessels to swear themselves bound for one of the English wool-ports and unload in France or Spain. By this means the trade in those ports is, in a great measure destroyed; and we were obliged to try our hands at finer works, having only our own consumption to depend on. And I can assure you we have, in several kinds of narrow goods, even exceeded the English, and, I believe, we shall in a few years more, be able to equal them in broad-cloths. But this you may depend upon, that scarce the tenth part of English goods are now imported of what used to be before the famous Act. The only manufactured wares we are allowed to export are linen cloth and linen yarn—which are marketable only in England. The rest of our commodities are —wool—restrained to England—and raw hides, skins, tallow, beef and butter. Now these are things for which the northern nations have no occasion; we are obliged therefore, instead of carrying woollen goods to their markets and bringing home money, to purchase their commodities. In France, Spain, and Portugal, our wares are more valuable, though it must be owned, our fraudulent trade in wool is the best branch of our commerce. From hence we get wines, brandy, and fruit, very cheap and in great perfection; so that though England has constrained us to be poor, they have given us leave to be merry. From these countries we bring home moidores, pistoles, and louisdores, without which we should scarce have a penny to turn upon.

"To England we are allowed to send nothing but linen cloth, yarn, raw hides, skins, tallow and wool. From thence we have coals, for which we always pay ready money, Indian goods, English woollen, and silks, tobacco, hardware, earthenware, salt and several other commodities. Our exportations to England are very much over-balanced by our importations, so that the course of exchange is generally too high, and people choose rather to make their remittances to England in specie, than by a bill, and our nation is perpetually drained of its little running cash."

Here are statements which, if they had appeared in a popular pamphlet—in a *Drapier's Letter*—might well be suspected of inaccuracy or exaggeration. But only bald facts would weigh with such a man as Walpole, who, moreover, had every means, and also every motive for detecting exaggeration or inaccuracy. As, therefore, no one ever calculated more nicely his range, his target, and the weight and sort of mettle needed to strike true than Swift, it may certainly be assumed that the strange statements in this letter were accurately and ascertainably true.

But surely they are strange, and even in some respects startling. To begin with, let us look at the extensiveness both of the manufacture and of the export of Irish woollens, broadcloths, druggets, bays and shalloons, worsted damasks, strong draught-works, sight half-works and gaudy stuffs, exported so extensively abroad that the current contemporary money of Ireland was foreign silver. All this industry and commerce were extirpated at one stroke out of shere English envy, and nothing else. "They looked with envious eyes upon our prosperity, and complained of being undersold by us *in those commodities which themselves did not deal in.*" They were not our competitors, nor were they even the beneficiaries of our bankruptcy. The trade eradicated here was transplanted, not to England, but to France, Spain, and the Netherlands, whither the exiled artizans carried the secret of the manufacture, and whither the Irish merchants smuggled its staple. Out of mere envy they robbed us of what not enriched them, but rather indirectly and considerably impoverished them. The extirpation of our trade cost England the loss of nine-tenths of her Irish customers. "You shall find English towns without one loom in them, which subsisted entirely upon the woollen manufactory before the passing of this unhappy Bill. ... Scarce the tenth part of English goods are now imported into Ireland of what used to be before the famous Act."

But, again, whose was this fine trade that was extirpated to the sole advantage of France, Spain, and the Netherlands? It was English and Scotch, and not Irish at all in any true sense. It was not the native Irish, but the English and Scotch settlers who were sacrificed with such wanton recklessness to the mere envy of their British brethren. The native Irish, politically degraded by the Penal Laws to the level of the cattle they were allowed to tend, had neither rights, property, nor freedom to be robbed of. No, it was at their masters, who had in their hands almost all the land and trade and commerce and manufactures of the country, that the successive measures for the extirpation of the industries of Ireland were aimed. To speak of these desolating measures as Irish grievances in the sense in which the Penal Laws were Irish grievances, is absurd. They were as fratricidal measures of Englishmen against Englishmen as the taxation which provoked the American Revolution. It was only indirectly that they affected the native Irish, and it is only indirectly and incidentally that Swift champions their cause. The robbery and oppression of the ascendency by England led to worse robbery and oppression of their tenantry by the ascendency. The landlords bullied and beggared, revenged themselves by bullying and beggaring their tenants, "as I," writes Swift, "when my betters give me a kick, am apt to revenge it with six kicks to my footman." This frightful oppression of the peasantry also, as we shall see, moved Swift to rage and remonstrance; but politically and commercially he fought only the battle of the Irish ascendency against the ascendency of England; and the sole ground of the quarrel was that Ireland was governed by and for Englishmen living in England, instead of by and for Englishmen living in Ireland. That the Scotch in the north of Ireland should have a voice in its government, Swift considered iniquitous, while he never considered at all, politically, the native Irish. Politically they were a negligeable quantity "as inconsiderable," to use his own words, "as their women and children." No doubt, that they became a political factor eventually was due as much to Swift as to any single man; but this was not in all his thoughts and most certainly not in all his wishes.

Thus the trade destroyed by England to the advantage of foreigners was substantially English, as, indeed, Swift insisted in an interview with

Walpole which remains on record in a letter to Lord Peterborough. The principal points he pressed in this interview were:—That almost every Irish trade and industry had been extirpated by England deliberately; That every Irish post of profit or importance was given to an Englishman; That the "Colonists," as he calls them, were thus robbed of their rights and property, which should have been respected as the rights and property of Englishmen whom emigration to Ireland had not denaturalized; That these impoverished and oppressed English colonists oppressed and impoverished in turn their tenants till, "the whole country, except the Scotch plantation in the North, was a scene of misery and desolation hardly to be matched on this side of Lapland;" That the result was such utter ruin to the country as must defeat the greed which caused it, since Ireland would soon be unable to yield to England the million a year tribute now extorted from it in one form or another. To this killing of the goose that laid the golden eggs point he returns in the letter as the one which alone was likely to weigh with Walpole. The country was being bled white and to death, he writes, and, if you do not regret the crime, you may yet have to regret the blunder you are committing. He then proceeds to point out through what various veins Ireland is being drained—a system of arterial drainage so perfect as to seem deliberately designed for her exhaustion. Significantly, however, he omits in the letter one channel of depletion which he dwelt on in the interview—that through which Walpole himself was draining the country's resources. As Walpole gave every office of profit to an Englishman, and as every Englishman who could, appointed a deputy at starvation wage to do his work, while he himself lived and spent the rest of his salary in England, the country did not get the advantage even of the money paid for its misgovernment. It was not uncommon for these incumbents, who had to take the oaths and the sacrament in Ireland upon their appointment to an Irish post, to make a visit—their first and their last—to this country of two clear days. Having landed on Saturday night at Ringsend, they took the sacrament on Sunday at the nearest church, the oaths in the courts on Monday morning, and in the afternoon of the same day re-embarked for England. Lastly, there was the Irish Pension List—a buck-basket into which every job too foul for exposure was flung—an infamous means for rewarding infamy. Of this foul pension-list and of these official absentees Swift says nothing in his letter to Walpole, because the abolition of such abuses could not be shown to be to the disadvantage of England. He could hope for the redress of such Irish grievances only as promised direct or indirect injury to England. Nevertheless he does refer in the letter to the evils of absenteeism, which at first sight might be supposed to bring to England the unmixed benefit of the expenditure in that country of a third of the total rental of Ireland. But up to the Revolution it had been the prudent and continuous policy of England to discourage Irish absenteeism in the interest of England herself. The Plantagenets, Tudors, and Stuarts alike imposed penalties of more or less severity upon Irish absentees, as upon the soldiers of a garrison who had deserted their post. By a statute of Richard II. two-thirds of the estate of an Irish absentee was forfeited to the Crown; while Henry VIII. resumed the whole of the estates of an habitual Irish absentee. As, however, Ireland, crushed to the earth, needed now no garrison, absenteeism, since it injured apparently only herself, had ceased to be penal. But did it injure, or promise to injure, herself alone? It was to this point Swift addressed himself, as to the sole consideration of weight with Walpole. By bleeding the wretched beast of burden you are overloading, he suggests, you may break it down till it is fit only for the knacker. It was in the hope of influencing Walpole by this consideration that Swift drew the following picture of the utter exhaustion of the country:—

"Another cause of the decay of trade, scarcity of money, and swelling of the exchange, is that universal affectation of our gentry to reside in and about London. Their rents are remitted to them and spent there. The countryman wants employment from them; the country shop-keeper wants their custom. For this reason he can't pay his Dublin correspondent readily, nor take off a great quantity of his wares. Therefore the Dublin merchant can't employ the artizan, nor keep up his credit in foreign markets.... Another great calamity is the exorbitant raising of the rent of lands. Upon the determination of all leases made before the year 1690, a gentleman thinks he has but indifferently improved his estate if he has only doubled his rent-roll. Farms are screwed up to a rack-rent; leases granted but for a small term of years; tenants tied down to hard conditions, and discouraged from cultivating the lands they occupy to the best advantage, by the certainty they have of their rent being raised on the expiration of their lease proportionately to the improvements they shall make. Thus is honest industry restrained; the farmer is a slave to his landlord; 'tis well if he can cover his family with a coarse home-spun frieze. The artizan has little dealings with him, yet he is obliged to take his provisions from him at an extravagant price, otherwise the farmer cannot pay his rent. The proprietors of lands keep great part of them in their own hands for sheep pasture; and there are thousands of poor wretches who think themselves blessed if they can obtain a hut worse than the squire's dog-kennel, and an acre of ground for a potato plantation, on condition of being as very a slave as any in America. What can be more deplorable than to behold wretches starving in the midst of plenty? We are apt to charge the Irish with laziness, because we seldom find them employed, but then we don't consider they have nothing to do."

Let us take together this letter and the interview recorded in that to Lord Peterborough, and what do we find? First, that Swift speaks principally as a "colonist"—as an Englishman living in Ireland, as the champion politically of what I may call the Church-of-England Ireland, to the exclusion of the Presbyterians, whom he detested, and of the Catholics, whom he scorned. Secondly, that it was not the trade of the native Irish, but that of the English and Scotch settlers, which was extirpated by their British brethren, and extirpated out of mere envy. Thirdly that the extirpation of this trade was so far from profiting, that it injured the English traders who instigated it, by the loss to them of nine-tenths of their Irish market. Fourthly, that to heap burdens upon Ireland with one hand, while, with the other, Walpole drained her life away, was as shortsighted as the Arab's drinking the blood of the camel upon whose endurance he depended to bear him to water.

But to all this Walpole turned a deaf ear, no doubt thinking what the bookseller in "Boswell" said of the hapless hack-writer, worn out in his beggarly service: "There's flesh on his bones yet!"

"One part of the Empire," says Macaulay, in his essay on Milton, "One part of the Empire," he sadly sighs, " was so unhappily circumstanced that at that time its misery was necessary to our happiness; its slavery to our freedom." It would be absurd, if it would not be even profane, for this part of the Empire, Ireland, to regret so slight a sacrifice in a cause so noble. "We Irish," writes Swift, "are ready to exclaim in the words of Cowley to his mistress,

'Forbid it, Heaven, my life should be
Weighed with her least conveniency!'"

As we are ready to give our vitals to poultice a scratch on your finger, we must needs contribute, even by our ruin, to the advantage, ever so trifling, of our superiors." But in Walpole's day we had not even the gratification of the sheep led to the slaughter of knowing that our sacrifice ministered to the happiness of a higher being. England did not benefit, and did not even seek her benefit, in our misery; she inflicted it in mere envy, and prolonged it in mere tyranny. Dr. Hugh Boulter, the Archbishop of Armagh, Walpole's virtual viceroy of Ireland for nineteen years, thanks the English Council for the rejection of a Bill aimed to promote an Irish manufacture, because "the rejection was not based *solely* on disregard of Ireland, but *also to some extent* on the notion that the rejection would benefit England." Disregard of the wishes and interests of Ireland, he admits, would alone be an adequate motive for the rejection by the Council of any Bill to her advantage; and the consideration of the Council in adding another motive for its rejection showed a graciousness that called for special acknowledgment! Has Swift in irony ever said anything more biting of the spirit of the English government of Ireland than what is suggested by the gratitude of Dr. Hugh Boulter?

Little wonder that Swift's appeal, though made by a colonist, for the colonists, to the mother country, was hopeless. He found what every Irishman who has ever won anything before or since for Ireland has found, that we must depend upon ourselves alone as the lever, and upon fear of revolt alone as the fulcrum for the moving of England for the redress of injustice. This lever and fulcrum Swift used in the tracts addressed to the Irish people, which I now proceed to consider.

CHAPTER VII.

SWIFT'S FIRST IRISH PAMPHLET.

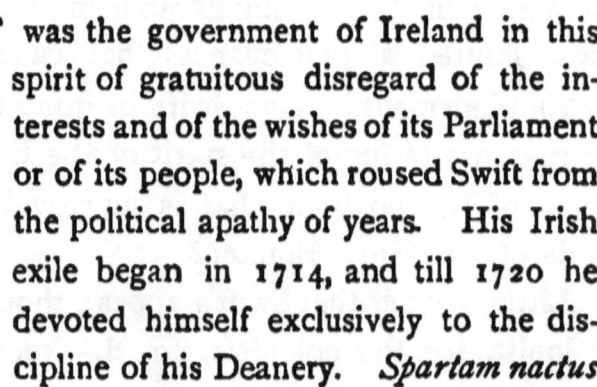T was the government of Ireland in this spirit of gratuitous disregard of the interests and of the wishes of its Parliament or of its people, which roused Swift from the political apathy of years. His Irish exile began in 1714, and till 1720 he devoted himself exclusively to the discipline of his Deanery. *Spartam nactus es; hanc exorna.* But all these years, however, "his heart was hot within him, and at last he spake with his tongue," and to some purpose. He tried in the year 1720 to rouse the Irish Parliament and people to make the only reprisal in their power against England by his tract, "A Proposal for the Universal Use of Irish Manufacture in Clothes and Furniture of Houses: Utterly Rejecting and Renouncing Everything Wearable that comes from England." In this masterly paper, Swift tells us the truth of all and to

all with a graphic vigour, which within less than a dozen pages, sets clearly before you what the state of Ireland was and who were responsible for its wretchedness and its ruin. The main, but far from the whole, responsibility rested on England:—

"The fable in Ovid of Arachne and Pallas is to this purpose: The goddess had heard of one Arachne, a young virgin, very famous for spinning and weaving. They both met upon a trial of skill; and Pallas, finding herself almost equalled in her own art, stung with rage and envy, knocked her rival down and turned her into a spider; enjoining her to spin and weave for ever out of her own bowels, and in a very narrow compass. I confess that from a boy I always pitied poor Arachne, and could never heartily love the goddess, on account of so cruel and unjust a sentence; which, however, is fully executed upon us by England, with farther additions of rigour and severity, for the greatest part of our bowels and vitals is extracted, without allowing us the liberty of spinning and weaving them. The Scripture tells us that "oppression makes a wise man mad;" therefore, consequently speaking, the reason why some men are not mad is because they are not wise. However, it were to be wished that oppression would in time teach a little wisdom to fools. I was much delighted with a person who has a great estate in this kingdom, upon his complaints to me, how grievously poor England suffers by impositions from Ireland:—that we convey our own wool to France, in spite of all the harpies at the Custom-house; that Mr. Shuttleworth and others on the Cheshire coasts, are such fools to sell us their bark at a good price for tanning our own hides into leather; with other enormities of the like weight and kind. To which I will venture to add more:—that the mayoralty of this city is always executed by an inhabitant, and often by a native, which might as well be done by a deputy with a moderate salary—whereby poor England loses at least one thousand pounds a year upon the balance: that the government of this kingdom costs the Lord Lieutenant £3,600 a year,—so much net loss to poor England; that the people of Ireland presume to dig for coals on their own grounds; that the farmers in the counties of Wicklow send their turf to the very market of Dublin, to the great discouragement of the coal trade of Mostyn and Whitehaven."

Sam Johnson once overheard a fishmonger cursing an eel he was skinning alive for attempting to wriggle away from the process; but Ireland, in attempting to establish a tanning trade, was even more inconsiderate, since, after being skinned alive, she was trying to grow a new skin.

But how was her Parliament helping her in the effort? Her Parliament, be it remembered, represented only a small minority of her people— only members of the Church of England. The Presbyterians of the north were as utter political outcasts as the Catholics of the South and West. This Parliament of a small and intolerant minority stood between England and Ireland precisely in the position in which a cringing and bullying agent stands between a rack-renting absentee landlord and his helpless and hopeless tenantry. Insolent towards Catholic and Presbyterian Ireland, towards England its attitude was abject.

"Nothing has humbled me so much, or shown a greater disposition to a contemptuous treatment of Ireland in some chief Governors than that high style of several speeches from the throne, delivered as usual, after the royal assent, in some periods of the two last reigns. Such exaggerations of the prodigious condescensions in the prince to pass those good laws would have but an odd sound at Westminster; neither do I apprehend how any good law can pass, wherein the King's interest is not as much concerned as that of the people. I remember after a speech on the like occasion delivered by my Lord Wharton (I think it was his last), he desired Mr. Addison to ask my opinion on it. My answer was:—'That his Excellency had very honestly forfeited his head on account of one paragraph, wherein he asserted by plain consequence, a dispensing power in the Queen." His Lordship owned it was true; but swore "The words were put into his mouth by direct orders from Court." Whence it was clear that some ministers in those times were apt, from their high elevation, to look down upon this kingdom as if it had been one of their colonies -of outcasts in America."

Passing from the Parliament to those it represented, in them also, and naturally, tyranny and servility went together, like the obverse and reverse of a coin.

"I would now expostulate a little with our country landlords, who, by unmeasurable screwing and racking their tenants all over the kingdom, have already reduced the people to a worse condition than the peasants of France, or the vassals in Germany and Poland; so that the whole species of what we call substantial farmers, will, in a very few years, be utterly at an end. It was pleasant to observe these gentlemen labouring with all their might for preventing the bishops from letting their revenues at a moderate half value (whereby the whole order would, in an age, have been reduced to manifest beggary), at the very instant when they were everywhere canting* their own land upon short leases, and sacrificing their oldest tenants for a penny an acre advance. I know not how it comes to pass (and yet, perhaps, I know well enough), that slaves have a natural disposition to be tyrants; and that when my betters give me a kick I am apt to revenge it with six upon my footman, although, perhaps, he may be an honest and diligent fellow. I have heard great divines affirm that nothing is so likely to call down a universal judgment upon a nation as universal oppression, and whether this be not verified in part, their worships, the landlords, are now at full leisure to consider. Whoever travels this country and observes the face of nature, or the faces and habits and dwellings of the natives, will hardly think himself in a land where law, religion, or common humanity is professed."

But, if the Irish Parliament and the Irish landlords had to share with England the responsibility for the extinction of Irish industries, so also in some degree had the people themselves and the shop-keepers.

"It is wonderful to observe the bias among our people in favour of things, persons, and wares of all kinds that come from England. The printer tells his hawkers

---

* "Canting," *i.e.*, auctioning, from French "quant," representing Latin "quantum."

that he has got an excellent new song, just brought from London. I have somewhat of a tendency that way myself, and upon hearing a coxcomb from thence displaying himself, with great volubility upon the park, the play-house, the opera, the gaming ordinaries, it was apt to beget in me a kind of reverence for his parts and accomplishments. It is not many years since I remember a person, who by his style and literature, seems to have been the corrector of a hedge-press in some blind-alley about Little Britain, proceed gradually to be an author, at least a translator of lower rate, although somewhat of a larger bulk, than any that now flourishes in Grubb Street; and upon the strength of this foundation, come over here, erect himself into an orator and politician, and lead a kingdom after him."

This Irish prejudice against Irish products lies deep down in the roots of our distracted history and seems to be ineradicable. What Swift says in another paper is as true to-day as when he wrote it:—

"Both sexes, but especially the women, despise and abhor to wear any of their own manufactures, even those which are better made than in other countries; particularly a sort of silk plaid, through which the workmen are forced to run a kind of gold thread, that it may pass for Indian. Even ale and potatoes are imported from England, as well as corn." In another Paper he enlarges upon a complaint he makes in this "Proposal for Use of Irish Manufacture" against the shop-keepers of "exacting and imposing upon the nobility and gentry, either as to the prices or the goodness of their wares."

"The mortal danger is, that if these dealers could prevail by the goodness and cheapness of their cloths and stuffs to give a turn to the principal people of Ireland in favour of their goods, they would relapse into the knavish practice, peculiar to this kingdom, which is apt to run through all trades, even so low as a common ale seller, who, as soon as he gets a vogue for his liquor and outsells his neighbour, thinks his credit will put off the worst he can buy till his customers will come no more."

Perhaps this short-sighted policy also persists among us to this day. A large employer of Irish labour said to me once, "An Irishman seems to me to regard the job in hand as the last he will ever get in this world, and to resolve to make all he can out of it without a thought of to-morrow." "We practise like peddlers," says Swift, "and sacrifice all honesty to the present urging advantage." A similar short-sightedness had something to do with an evil at least as prevalent in our day as it was in Swift's—the depopulation of the country through the substitution of pasturage for tillage.

"It is the peculiar felicity and prudence of the people of this kingdom," he says sarcastically at the opening of this 'Proposal,' "that whatever commodities and productions lie under the greatest discouragements from England, those are what they are sure to be most industrious in cultivating and spreading. Agriculture. which has been the principal care of all wise nations, and for the encouragement whereof there are so many statute laws in England, we countenance so well, that the landlords are everywhere by penal clauses absolutely prohibiting their tenants from ploughing—not satisfied to confine them within certain limitations, as is the practise of the English. One effect of which is already seen in the prodigious dearness of corn, and the importation of it from London, as the cheaper market. And because people are the riches of a country, and that our neighbours have done, and are doing, all that in them lies to make our wool a drug to us, and a monopoly to them; therefore the politic gentlemen of Ireland have depopulated vast tracts of the best land in Ireland for the feeding of sheep."

In another Paper—"Answer to a Memorial"—he

writes with as much wit as wisdom, "Ajax was mad when he mistook a flock of sheep for his enemies; but we shall never be sober, until we have the same way of thinking."

But distracted and demoralized as the country was, she had a common enemy and common interests, and one hope of the recovery of her extinguished trade; and this was the inspiration of Swift's vigorous appeal:

"I could wish the Parliament had thought fit to have suspended their regulation of Church matters, and enlargements of the prerogative, until a more convenient time, because they did not appear very pressing, at least to the persons principally concerned; and, instead of these great refinements in politics and divinity, had amused themselves and their committees a little with the state of the nation. For example: What if the House of Commons had thought fit to make a resolution, *nemine contradicente*, against wearing any cloth or stuff in their families, which were not of the growth and manufacture of this kingdom? What if they had extended it so far as utterly to exclude all silks, velvets, callicoes, and the whole lexicon of female fopperies, and declared that whoever acted otherwise should be deemed and reputed an enemy to the nation? What if they had sent up such a resolution to be agreed to by the House of Lords, and by their own practise and encouragement spread the execution of it in their several countries? What if we should agree to make burying in woollen a fashion, as our neighbours have made it a law? What if the ladies would be content with Irish stuffs for the furniture of their houses, for gowns and petticoats for themselves and their daughters? Upon the whole, and to crown all the rest, let a firm resolution be taken by male and female never to appear with one single shred that comes from England, and let all the people say, 'AMEN!' I hope and believe nothing could please his Majesty better than to hear that his loyal subjects of both sexes in the kingdom celebrated his birthday (now approaching) universally clad in their own manufacture. Is there virtue enough left in this deluded people to save them from the brink of ruin? If men's opinions may be taken, the ladies will look as handsome in stuffs as in brocades; and, since all will be equal, there may be room enough to employ their wit and fancy in choosing and matching patterns and colours. I heard the late Archbishop of Tuam mention a pleasant observation of somebody's—'that Ireland would never be happy till a law were made for burning everything that came from England, except their people and their coals.' I must confess that, as to the former, I should not be sorry if they would stay at home; and, for the latter, I hope in a little time we shall have no occasion for them:—

'Non tanti mitra est, non tanti judicis ostrum.'

But I should rejoice to see a staylace from England be thought scandalous and become a topic of censure at visits and tea-tables."

Here then is the famous tract, word for word, and almost every word—not on the face of it, you would say, "a seditious, factious, and virulent libel." Nevertheless it was held to be so, not by the English Government only, and not only by their usual Irish instrument of tyranny, a Lord Chief Justice, but even by two Irish Grand Juries! That Chief Justice Whitshed should have strained every nerve and every point to secure a conviction was natural—in Ireland. The usual stepping-stone to the Irish Bench is the trampled body of Justice, and a lawyer who owes his promotion to unscrupulous political partizanship, cannot change, but only cover, the skin of the Ethiopian with the ermine of the judge. But that the Grand Juries both of the city and of the county of Dublin should bring in a True Bill—present Swift's tract as "a seditious, factious, and virulent libel"—is much to the credit of his fellow "colonists." The petty Jury was not so timid, or so complaisant; since it was only after Whitshed had detained it eleven hours, and had sent it back nine times to reconsider its acquittal, that it was worried and wearied into bringing in a special verdict which would allow the case to be re-tried. But "the person in great office" who had intimated to Whitshed that he must procure a conviction at all costs, and the Chief Justice who had tried to procure it at the cost of a judicial scandal so gross as to shock even the Government ring, had overshot the mark. The public conscience was so revolted that the re-trial was postponed from term to term, until the coming of the Duke of Grafton as Viceroy gave Whitshed and his accomplice, Judge Boate, the opportunity of a discreet retreat under cover of a *nolle prosequi*.

Nothing proves the need of this tract better than the prosecution of its printer. Swift in it aimed as much at the revival of the spirit of the country as at the revival of its trade; and the need of the revival of the spirit of the country may be measured by the servility of these juries under the crack of the whip of this English Pacha, Whitshed.

CHAPTER VIII.

First "Drapier's Letter."

SWIFT'S "Proposal for the Universal Use of Irish Manufacture" aimed to revive, not the extinguished trade only, but the extinguished spirit also, of the "colonists." The presentation of it by two Grand Juries as a "seditious, factious and virulent libel" is some measure of the need of such an appeal; the dogged evasion of a conviction by a Petty Jury is some measure of its success. Both juries were composed exclusively of those "colonists" in whose exclusive interests the appeal was made; for what trade there was, or had been, in the country was almost wholly in their hands. Yet this appeal made specially to them and for them was answered in one case by a neutral, and in the other two cases by a damnatory verdict. The most deadly consequence of slavery is the servility it breeds, till backs long bowed beneath its load cannot be straightened. That is a fine comparison of Campanella's of a people habituated to servitude to an animal habituated to domestication; and the truth with which it closes—that such a people on a summons to shake off the yoke, turns to rend, not the oppressor, but the liberator—is exemplified in every history, and by the lives of many liberators from Moses to Swift:

> "The people is a beast of muddy brain
>   That knows not its own strength, and therefore stands
>   Loaded with wood and stone; the powerless hands
>   Of a mere child guide it with bit and rein;
> One kick would be enough to break the chain;
> But the beast fears, and what the child demands
> It does; nor its own terror understands,
> Confused and stupefied by bugbears vain.
> Most wonderful! With its own hand it ties
> And gags itself—gives itself death and war
> For pence doled out by kings from its own store.
> Its own are all things between earth and heaven;
> But this it knows not; and, if one arise
> To tell this truth, it kills him unforgiven."

But the most abject and inveterate servility is bred, not of slavery alone, but of tyranny and slavery wedded together; for at heart there is no such cringeing slave as a slave-driver. Hence, in Ireland the class represented by the Grand Juries of the city and of the county of Dublin, was as abject towards England as it was arrogant at home—a dog that licked its master's hand with a tongue red with the blood of the hunt. The eagerness, therefore, of these two Grand Juries to turn and rend their benefactor at the bidding of England was really less surprising than the hesitation of the Petty Jury to pronounce his patriotism a crime. Swift had to appeal to a wider and less spaniel-spirited constituency, and to appeal to it in the trumpet tones of the *The Drapier's Letters*, before he could rouse the country from its apathy of despair. But, meanwhile, he developed an attack he had begun at the close of his " Proposal for the Universal Use of Irish Manufacture," upon a project then pressed on the Parliament for the establishment of a National Bank.

"I cannot forbear," he writes, at the close of this tract, "saying one word upon a thing they call a bank, which, I fear, is projecting in this town. What I wish for at present, is only a sufficient provision of hemp and caps and bells, to distribute according to the several degrees of honesty and prudence in some persons. I hear only of a monstrous sum already named; and, if others do not hear of it soon, and hear with a vengeance, then I am a gentleman of less sagacity than myself, and very few beside myself, take me to be. And the jest will be still the better if it be true, as judicious persons have assured me, that one half of this money will be real, and the other half imaginary. The matter will be likewise much mended, if the merchants continue to carry off our gold, and our goldsmiths to melt down our heavy silver."

Here he opens the lines of an assault which he followed up in other tracts with such spirit and success that Parliament rejected the project.

There are, I understand, even to-day some who doubt if the Irish banks, which are mere reservoirs for the irrigation of foreign enterprises and industries with Irish money, are an unmixed benefit; but in Swift's day such a doubt was even more defensible. The projected bank was but one of a hundred wild schemes then afloat, of which I may cite as a specimen that for the introduction of a breed of asses—probably an indispensable preparatory provision for the success of subsequent speculations of the kind. The promoters of this bank were, in fact, a few stock-brokers of no commercial standing, fore-runners of those modern wreckers, the company promoters. The extinction of this project by pouring upon it perhaps disproportionate ridicule was the only work of importance Swift did for Ireland between the issue in 1720 of the "Proposal for the Universal Use of Irish Manufacture" and the first of the epoch-making *Drapier's Letters*, which appeared in 1724.

The Drapier's Letters are epoch-making in that they first taught Ireland the policy and the power of union, of dogged inert resistance, and of strategically organized and directed agitation. Their effect was, in fact, commensurate with their power, and their power of its kind was supreme. It is the power of a deft, vigorous, intent and unerring-eyed wielder of a hammer, who hits each nail on the head and home without one single feint, or flourish, or one single short, or wide, or weak, or wasted stroke. Swift's consummate mastery of the art which conceals art was never shown to such perfection as in these Letters, whose naked simplicity is so like naked truth as to be confounded with it. Yet there was about as much naked truth in them as in *Gulliver's Travels!* More singular than the power, or even than the effect of these unique *Letters* is their disingenuousness. It is inconceivable to me that Swift's admirers can credit their own contention—that he objected to Wood's Halfpence on the grounds assigned by the *Drapier;* or even that he thought these grounds of objection valid. One of the most urgent wants of Ireland at this time—as Swift admits—was a lack of small change. This lack Wood would have supplied with a copper coinage of absolutely twice the intrinsic value of the bronze coinage current in the country to-day. As there is no such economical heresy as tri-mettalism, Swift must have known that the copper coinage of any country are as mere counters as bank-paper; and if he did not know it, he had the re-assurance of Wood's patent itself, that no one need take in any one payment more than five-pence half-penny of his coin. This, of course, meant that any sum of the value of the silver or the gold currency should be paid in silver or gold, and only sums below the level of this currency were legally payable in Wood's halfpence. It is not for a moment supposable that Swift believed copper was henceforth in Ireland alone of the countries in the world to be made as legal tender as gold for sums to any amount. Yet he proceeds altogether and with circumstantial and telling detail upon this really preposterous assumption :—

"The common weight of these halfpence is between four and five to an ounce—suppose five; then, three shillings and four pence will weigh a pound, and consequently twenty shillings will weigh six pounds butter weight. Now, there are many hundred farmers who pay two hundred pounds a year rent; therefore, when one of these farmers comes with his half year's rent—which is one hundred pounds—it will be at least six hundred pounds' weight, which is three horses' load. If a squire has a mind to come to town to buy clothes and wine and spices for himself and family, or perhaps to pass the winter here, he must bring with him five or six horses, well loaded with sacks, as the farmers bring their corn; and when his lady comes in her coach to our shops, it must be followed by a car loaded with Mr. Wood's money. And I hope we shall have the grace to take it for no more than it is worth. They say Squire Connolly "—Speaker of the Irish House of Commons—" has sixteen thousand pounds a year; now, if he sends for his rent to town, as it is likely he does, he must have two hundred and fifty horses to bring up his half-year's rent, and two or three great cellars in his house for stowage. But what the bankers will do, I cannot tell; for I am assured that some great bankers keep by them forty thousand pounds in ready cash, to answer all payments—which sum, in Mr. Wood's money—would require twelve hundred horses to carry it."

The only adequate parallel to this elaborate calculation is that made with, no doubt, equal seriousness, in *Gulliver's Travels*, of the number, size, and weight of the chains and padlocks designed by the Emperor of Lilliput for the perpetual bondage of Gulliver.

But in the second *Drapier's Letter* Swift is forced to face this provision in the patent that no one need take in any one payment more than five-pence halfpenny of Wood's coin. How does he face it? By assuming that no one need take more than five-pence halfpenny of this coin in any single payment, means that everyone must take as much in every single payment. He faces it, that is, by the assumption, that the coin was intended, not as change, but as a tax of five-pence halfpenny on each transaction, small and great for the enrichment of Mr. Wood; and that in some mysterious way *both* parties in each transaction—the payer no less than the payee—would be losers to the extent of seventeen shillings in the pound!

"His proposals conclude with perfect high treason. He promises that no person shall be obliged to receive more than five-pence halfpenny of his coin in one payment. By which it is plain that he pretends to oblige every subject in this kingdom to take so much in every payment if it be offered; whereas his patent obliges no man, nor can the prerogative, by law, claim such a power, as I have often observed. So that here Mr. Wood takes upon him the entire legislature, and an absolute dominion over the properties of the whole nation. Good God! Who are this wretch's advisers? Who are his supporters, abettors, encouragers, or sharers? Mr. Wood will oblige me to take five-pence halfpenny of his brass in every payment; and I will shoot Mr. Wood and his deputies through the head, like highwaymen or housebreakers, if they dare to force one farthing of their coin on me in the payment of a hundred pounds. It is no loss of honour to submit to the lion; but who with the figure of a man, can think with patience of being devoured alive by a rat? He has laid a tax upon the people of Ireland of seventeen shillings, at least, in the pound—a tax, I say, not only on lands, but interest-money, goods, manufactures, the hire of handicraftsmen, labourers, and servants. Shopkeepers, look to yourselves! Wood will oblige and force you to take five-pence halfpenny of his trash in every payment; and many of you receive twenty, thirty, forty payments in one day, or else you can hardly find bread. And pray, consider how much that will amount to in a year. Twenty times five-pence halfpenny is nine shillings and two pence, which is above a hundred and sixty pounds a year; wherein you will be losers of at least one hundred and forty pounds by taking your payments in his money. If any of you be content to deal with Mr. Wood on such conditions you may. But, for my own particular, let his money perish with him. If the famous Mr. Hampden rather chose to go to prison than pay a few shillings to King Charles I. without authority of Parliament, I will rather chose to be hanged than have all my substance taxed at seventeen shillings in the pound, at the arbitrary will and pleasure of the venerable Mr. Wood."

That the shop-keepers, handicraftsmen, labourers, and servants should believe that the currency of Wood's coin would mean a tax levied by this iron-monger of five-pence halfpenny on every transaction, and of seventeen shillings in every pound, is sufficiently astonishing, though sufficiently established. No man ever calculated more nicely his charge, his distance, and his target, than Swift, and that he should overshoot his audience's credulity in this instance, is antecedently improbable; while it is historically certain that his shot told as never shot of the kind had told before. Therefore, we cannot doubt that Swift's elaborate and preposterous perversions of the intention and of the operation of Wood's scheme really were swallowed by his intelligent audience. But that they imposed on Swift himself is not incredible only, but inconceivable. Why, then, did the sincerest and least histrionic of men resort to this disingenuous clap-trap? In part, it must be admitted, but only in small part, because he was playing to the gallery—making to the people within and without the Pale the only appeal that would heat and fuse them together. But chiefly he made this *ad captandum vulgus* appeal because it was the only one possible to make with impunity. If he had opposed and exposed the real iniquity of this scandalous and insolent project, his printer—if he could have found a printer—would have been punished by something worse than imprisonment.

"About four years ago," he writes, in the first DRAPIER'S LETTER, "a little book was written to advise all people to wear the manufacture of this our own dear country. It had no other design; said nothing against the King or Parliament, or any persons whatever; yet the poor printer was prosecuted two years with the utmost violence, and even some weavers themselves (for whose sake it was written) being upon the jury, found him guilty. This would be enough to discourage any man from endeavouring to do you good, when you will either neglect him, or fly in his face for his pains, and when he must expect only danger to himself, and to be fined and imprisoned, perhaps to his ruin."

If the "Proposal for the Universal Use of Irish Manufacture," whose political inoffensiveness is here fairly defined, narrowly escaped conviction of being "a seditious, factious and virulent libel," what would have been the fate of a tract which opened, let us say, by quoting a Charter dating from Richard III. :—"Hibernia habet parliamentum et faciunt leges: et nostra statuta non ligant eos, quia non mittunt milites ad parliamentum;" which proceeded then to show that for thirty years Ireland had been governed as a conquered province by the Parliament of England with insolent disregard to every petition and protest of her own Parliament; and which concluded with the secret history of the culminating instance of this insolent tyranny—Wood's patent?

What was that history? "The lean dog is all fleas," says a Spanish proverb; and in these days exhausted Ireland was bled white by a swarm of parasites pensioned upon her establishment. Among the rest figured the honoured name of the King's German mistress, the Duchess of Kendal, whose services to the country were gratefully acknowledged by pensions upon the Irish establishment to the amount of £3,000 a year. Thinking the acknowledgment inadequate she demanded and received this patent for the supply of copper coinage to Ireland, and sold it to one William Wood, a hardware man for £10,000. The assent of the Irish Houses of Parliament is not asked, their dissent is disregarded. The two Irish Houses of Parliament, the Privy-council, the Lord Mayor and aldermen of Dublin, and of other Corporations, the Grand Juries and the principal gentlemen of every county in Ireland protested and petitioned in vain. The courteous reply was, in the words of one of the English Ministers, "we will cram the brass down their throats." Why? The answer is the answer also to the question, why England has failed in Ireland. The coin was needed, was good, and was imposed by England, and there was no more to be said. As to the origin of the patent—*non olet;* as to the manner of its imposition—*non uti libet, sed uti licet.* National sensibility and sensitiveness were negligeable, or unintelligible rather, characteristics and considerations. "Ireland," says Carlyle, "is a gentleman thrown into the workhouse," and Bumble, the beadle, is at once perplexed and enraged by his squeamishness. "What have you to complain of? Have you not a roof over you, and a bed under you, and warm workhouse frieze and flannel to clothe you, and "gruel thick, and slab" to feed you? I can't understand————." "Ah, that is what I have to complain of," sighs the decayed gentleman, "You cannot understand." The foul origin of the patent, or the brutal cramming of the brass down the nation's throat were inconsiderable sentimentalities compared with the convenience, the goodness and the lawfulness of the coinage. But this standpoint of the unimaginative, unsympathetic and overbearing Bumble, is not the standpoint of the decayed gentleman whom fortune has flung under his feet. Hence the continual friction of "incompatibility," to use Mathew Arnold's phrase for our ill-assorted union, and hence much, if not most, of the eternal Irish difficulty. A single, but a convincing instance of this narrow, hard and rasping English handling of the matter may suffice. The latest of Swift's biographers, the most cultivated and liberal of Englishmen, thus comments upon the compensation of £24,000 made to Wood for the withdrawal of the patent, when dread of a rebellion at last compelled its withdrawal. "The conclusion is in one respect rather absurd. The Irish succeeded in rejecting a real benefit at the cost of paying Wood the profit which he would have made, had he been allowed to confer it." Absurd to tear down the flag of an invader, if you have afterwards to pay the cost of the bunting! It is only fair to quote also the subsequent admission of this biographer that "the very essence of the case was that the Irish people were to be plundered by the German mistress." But even this view is narrow and shortsighted and overlooks what, indeed, is almost always overlooked in taking account of the extent and of the success of a popular agitation—that it is not the match or the kindling which makes a conflagration, but the long-accumulated fuel. The *Drapier's Letters* was the match; the foulness of the origin and the insolence of the imposition of Wood's halfpence was the inflammable kindling, but thirty years of oppression and plunder, of the sacrifice of every Irish interest and industry, of the ostracism of every Irishman from every Irish preferment, of gratuitous disregard of every Irish wish and want, solely, to quote again from Archbishop Boulter, *because* it was Irish, this was the long-accumulated fuel. Hence the success of the *Drapier's Letters*. That the minting of the coin of a kingdom—an imperial privilege—should be sold to an ironmonger by a German concubine, who received it as a supplement to wages of her infamy —already paid by Ireland—was but the culminating insult of a series without a break, and without the prospect of a break. It would not, gross as it was, alone account for the intense, though flameless, glow of the *Drapier's Letters*, nor for their effect in firing Ireland from end to end instantaneously and irresistibly. White-hot with the exasperation of a thousand national insults and injuries, they were thrust into fuel which years had heaped high. We must keep this continually in mind, if we would adequately estimate the spirit which inspired these Letters and the spirit which they roused. And we must also remember that in rousing this spirit Swift had to walk and work warily. If, as he himself says, the "Proposal for the Universal Use of Irish Manufacture" was held treasonous, what would be the penalty exacted for a trumpet call to Ireland to form in solid square of inert resistance?

At first, therefore, and until he had felt the pulse

of his public and found that it beat as high as his own, Swift had to pretend the quarrel was with Wood and not with England, and about the quality and the conditions of the coinage, and not about the baseness of its origin and the tyranny of its imposition. In the later Letters, as we shall see, he was emboldened by the backing of a solid Ireland, to base his case more broadly and soundly, though even in these he never ventured to expose the *terrima belli causa*. But, then, of this there was no need, since the scandal, being of the swiftest-winged kind of all, had already reached the remotest corner of Ireland.

CHAPTER IX.

FOURTH "DRAPIER'S LETTER."

HE Statesman who take the occasion of an international quarrel for its cause, is as common and as shallow an empiric as the quack who takes an eruptive symptom for the long and deep-seated disease which it indicates. This mistake English statesmen are continually making in Ireland, in part, through arrogance, in part, through unimaginativeness, and, in part through the hand-to-mouth exigencies of party government. In the case of the universal rejection by Ireland of Wood's coinage, it was chiefly arrogance which blinded the English Ministers to the real reasons for a stand so dogged and solid. In the very wording of the Report of the Committee of the Eng-

lish Privy Council upon Wood's halfpence, this arrogance parades itself. In that report, the opposition to the coinage of the Irish Privy Council and Parliament of the two Houses of Lords and Commons, of the Municipalities, Grand Juries, of all the representatives of the Nation, and of the Nation itself, is styled "a clamour."

"The addresses of the Lords and Commons of Ireland against a ruinous destructive project of an obscure single undertaker," writes Swift in his third DRAPIER'S LETTER, "is called a 'clamour!' I desire to know how such a style would be resented in England from a committee of the Privy Council there to a Parliament; and how many impeachments would follow upon it?"

In truth, this Committee of the English Privy Council no more concerned itself with the rights, reasons, or feelings of the Irish or their representatives, than Mrs. Squeers regarded those of the boys she dosed with brimstone and treacle. If the brimstone and treacle were good, and good for them, then it mattered nothing whether they liked it, or liked the manner in which it was thrust down their throats by an odious harpy, in a common and a filthy spoon. The need of the coinage was urgent, and its quality was fair, and these were the sole considerations of moment. That it should be thrust down the throat of Ireland by the King's mistress, and through this low ironmonger Wood, were negligeable considerations; and negligeable also was the consideration that the circumstances of the imposition of the coinage, and the imposition itself, were in keeping with the "Do-the-boys Hall" misgovernment of Ireland for a generation. In fact, "the clamour" of Ireland against the coinage, and the English contempt of that clamour, sprang from the same source—thirty years of high-handed tyranny which had encouraged English arrogance, and exhausted Irish endurance. It never now occurred to an English Minister to consult Ireland, even as to the sauce wherein she was to be cooked, upon which, at least, the doomed chickens in the French apologue were allowed to venture an opinion.

Wood's halfpence, then, were rather the occasion than the cause of a volcanic outburst of long-pent discontent, and were less resented and resisted as in themselves an intolerable grievance than as a symbol and a sample of a long series of intolerable grievances. In the third *Drapier's Letter*, Swift suggests this by supposing Ireland's case to be England's own:—

"Put the case that the two houses of Lords and Commons of England and the Privy Council there should address his Majesty to recall a patent, from whence they apprehended the most ruinous consequences to the whole kingdom; and, to make it stronger, if possible, that the whole nation almost to a man, should thereupon discover 'the most dismal apprehensions,' as Mr. Wood styles them; would his Majesty debate half an hour what he had to do? Would any Minister dare to advise him against recalling such a patent? Or would the matter be referred to the Privy Council, or to Westminster Hall—the two Houses of Parliament, plaintiffs, and William Wood, defendant! And is there even the smallest difference between the two cases? Were not the people of Ireland born as free as those in England? How have they forfeited their freedom? Is not their Parliament as fair a representative of the people as that of England? And has not their Privy Council as great, or greater share in the administration of public affairs? Are not they subjects of the same king? Does not the same sun shine upon them? And have they not the same God for their protector? Am I a freeman in England, and do I become a slave in six hours in crossing the channel?"

But it was in the fourth *Drapier's Letter* that Swift, with the courage of a watch-dog, who sees at last at his back the master he had succeeded in rousing, lifts up and plants the question upon its proper national plane :—

"This gives me the opportunity of explaining to those who are ignorant, another point which has often swelled in my breast. Those who come over hither to us from England, and some weak people among ourselves, whenever in discourses we make mention of liberty and property, shake their heads, and tell us that Ireland is a depending kingdom, as if they would seem by this phrase to intend that the people of Ireland are in some state of slavery or dependence different from those of England; whereas a depending kingdom is a modern term of art, unknown, as I have heard, to all ancient civillians and writers upon government; and Ireland is, on the contrary, called in some statutes, 'an imperial crown,' as held only from God, which is as high a style as any kingdom is capable of receiving. Therefore, by the expression, 'a depending kingdom,' there is no more to be understood than that, by a statute made here in the thirty-third year of Henry VIII., the king and his successors are to be kings imperial of this realm, as united and knit to the imperial crown of England. I have looked over all English and Irish statutes without finding any law that makes Ireland depend upon England, any more than England does upon Ireland. We have, indeed, obliged ourselves to have the same king with them, and consequently they are obliged to have the same king with us. For the law was made by our own Parliament, and our ancestors then were not such fools (whatever they were in the preceding reign) to bring themselves under I know not what dependence, which is now talked of, without any ground of law, reason, or common sense. Let whoever thinks otherwise, I, M. B. Drapier, desire to be excepted; for I declare, next under God, I depend only on the king, my sovereign, and on the laws of my own country. And I am so far from depending upon the people of England, that if ever they should rebel against my sovereign (which God forbid!) I would be ready, at the first command from his majesty, to take arms against them, as some of my countrymen did against theirs at Preston. And if such a rebellion should prove so successful as to fix the Pretender on the throne of England, I would venture to transgress that statute so far as to lose every drop of my blood to hinder him from being King of Ireland."

May I intervene here to say that this passage, which was specially relied upon afterwards to secure the conviction of the printer of the paper, was evidently and ingeniously meant rather to be defensive than defiant. Swift, be it always remembered, wrote as the representative of that narrow Church-of-England Ireland, bounded on one side by the Penal Laws from the Catholics, and, on the other side, by the Test Act from the Presbyterians. "Is not our Parliament," he asks in the third 'Letter,' "as fair a representative of the people as that of England?" That is, it as fairly represented the Church of England in one country as in the other; but while the bulk of the people in England, was thereby represented, the Irish Parliament represented only a minute fraction, of the Irish nation. Now, the English press, in order to discredit the agitation against the coinage in the most effective way conceivable, declared it to be of exclusively Catholic origin and propagation. This misrepresentation, Swift, in the opening of the fourth "Letter," indignantly denies, and his denial is worth quoting as defining the Protestant limit of his patriotism sufficiently sharply :—

"Wood prescribes to the newsmongers in London what they are to write. In one of their papers, published here by some obscure printer, and certainly with a bad design, we are told, 'That the Papists in Ireland have entered into an association against his coin,' although it be notoriously known that they never once offered to stir in the matter; so that the two Houses of

Parliament, the Privy Council, the great number of Corporations, the Lord Mayor, and aldermen of Dublin, the Grand Juries and principal gentlemen of several counties are stigmatized in a lump under the name of 'Papists.'"

In his declaration, then, that "he would lose every drop of his blood to hinder the Pretender from being King of Ireland," Swift was not only repudiating the charge of Jacobitism, but protesting that on this point he was a stauncher Whig than the Whigs themselves—as he was. But he was a Whig in this, and only in this, and only because, to use his own intolerant illustration, though the Whigs might let loose at his Church "an angry cat," *i.e.*, the Presbyterians, they kept the Catholics at her foot like "a lion fast bound with three or four chains, his teeth drawn out and his claws pared to the quick." Nevertheless, the Irish Catholics, knowing that Swift fought and beat their common enemy, stood staunchly by him when his own set and side deserted him. Fifteen years later he writes to Pope that "as he walks the streets he has a thousand hats and blessings upon old scores which those we call the gentry have forgot." And well he deserved this recognition, for he was the pioneer of a mode of warfare to which the Catholics owe what they have, and look to what they hope for, of religious and political freedom. It was Swift taught them to return upon England the only argument England has ever stooped either to address to Ireland, or to attend to in appeals addressed by Ireland to her. This argument Swift describes in the next paragraph of the " Letter " :—

"It is true, indeed, that within the memory of man, the Parliaments of England have sometimes assumed the power of binding this kingdom by laws enacted there; wherein they were at first openly opposed (as far as truth, reason, and justice are capable of opposing) by the famous Mr. Molineux, an English gentleman born here, as well as by several of the greatest patriots and best Whigs in England; but the love and torrent of power prevailed. Indeed, the arguments on both sides were invincible. For, in reason, all government without the consent of the governed is the very definition of slavery; but, in fact, eleven men, well armed will certainly subdue one single man in his shirt."

Ireland, it is true, has always had the advantage in armour of England, poetically :—

"Thrice is he armed that hath his quarrel just,"

But the power which is on the side of the big battalions, laughs at this air-woven armour of poetry. Accordingly the eleven men well-armed would hold down for ever the single man in his shirt, in spite of the armour wherewith the poets—like the rascally tailors in "The Emperor's New Clothes"—have equipped him, but for two things. First, the distraction of foreign English quarrels, and, secondly, the distraction of internal English divisions, which render either the neutrality or the alliance of the single man in his shirt worth purchase by England at the price of some concession, which Justice had asked for, and would for ever have asked for in vain.

But there is something besides this distraction at home or abroad of the eleven armed men needed to gain for the man in his shirt this concession—the spirit to press for it determinedly—and this spirit Swift, in the next paragraph, proceeds to rouse :—

"And as we are apt to sink too much under unreasonable fears, so we are too soon inclined to be raised by groundless hopes, according to the nature of all consumptive bodies like ours. Thus, it has been given about for several days past, that somebody in England had empowered a second somebody to write to a third somebody here, to assure us that we should no more be troubled with these halfpence. And this is reported to have been done by the same person who is said to have sworn some months ago, 'that he would ram them down our throats,' though I doubt they would stick in our stomachs. But whichever of these reports be true or false is no concern of ours. For, in this point we have nothing to do with English ministers, and I should be sorry to leave it in their power to redress this grievance, or to enforce it; for the report of the Committee has given me a surfeit. The remedy is wholly in your own hands, and therefore I have digressed a little, in order to refresh and continue that spirit so seasonably raised among you, and to let you see that by the laws of GOD, of NATURE, of NATIONS, and of your COUNTRY, you ARE, and OUGHT to be as FREE a people as your brethren in England."

The capitals are in the original and indicate mechanically what in Swift's own view was the real point in dispute in the "Letters" and between the countries —the freedom of the little Ireland of "colonists" from English oppression. This spirited fourth "Letter" forced the Irish agents of this oppression to recognize it also as the real *casus belli*, and they therefore issued a proclamation offering a reward of £300 for the discovery of the author of the "Drapier's Fourth Letter," and describing it as

"A wicked and malicious pamphlet, containing several seditious and scandalous passages, highly reflecting upon his majesty and his ministers, and tending to alienate the affections of his good subjects in England and Ireland from each other."

Hard upon the issue of the proclamation followed the imprisonment of the printer of the "Letter,"—Harding, the forgotten martyr of the quarrel—an act of petty persecution Swift resented so openly as to leave no one in doubt as to the authorship of the "Letter." At the levée next day he elbowed his way up to the

Lord Lieutenant—Lord Carteret, a personal friend—and thundered :—

"So my Lord, this is a glorious exploit you performed yesterday in suffering a proclamation against a poor shopkeeper, whose only crime is an honest endeavour to save his country from ruin. I suppose your lordship will expect a statue in copper for your services to Mr. Wood?"

To which Lord Carteret, who had but just assumed office, made the good-tempered reply of an apt quotation from Virgil :—

"Res dura, et regni novitas me talia cogunt Moliri."

A rejoinder so happy as to seem to everyone—except, perhaps, to Harding—to make up for the harshness of the measure it extenuated.

Again, in a letter written upon the issue of the proclamation to its issuer, Lord Chancellor Midleton, Swift virtually acknowledges himself the incriminated "Drapier"; but legal proof he was careful not to give. He employed his butler, Robert Blakeley, to copy the "Letters" and to convey them to the printer, and he summarily dismissed him on his absenting himself from the Deanery one evening without leave. He was not going, he said, to keep a servant who was emboldened to neglect his duties by the consciousness of having his master in his power. "Strip off your livery, begone from the Deanery instantly, and do the worst to revenge yourself that you dare to do!" The man, more hurt by the suspicion which caused his dismissal than by the harshness of the dismissal itself, revenged himself by an inviolable secrecy as to the reason of his discharge. When the danger had blown over Swift sent for Blakeley, and summoned at the same time all the other Deanery servants to whom he thus re-introduced his late butler:—"This is no longer your fellow-servant, Robert, the butler, but Mr. Blakeley, verger of St. Patrick's, a post which his integrity has obtained him."

There is a magnanimity about this dismissal of Blakeley which to me seems inconsistent with Swift's supposed meanness in allowing Harding to lie in jail. Swift has been charged with acting somewhat in the spirit he satirises in the delightfully humorous story of the Madrid Jew.

"I was, in a manner," he writes in another 'Drapier's Letter,' "left alone to stand the battle; while others, who had ten thousand times better talents than a Drapier, were so prudent as to lie still; and perhaps thought it no unpleasant amusement to look on with safety, while another was giving them diversion at the hazard of his liberty and fortune, and thought they made sufficient recompense by a little applause. Like the Jew at Madrid, who, being condemned to the fire on account of his religion, a crowd of school-boys following him to the stake, and apprehending that they might lose their sport if he should happen to recant, would often clap him on the back and cry 'Sta firme, Moyse;' 'Moses, continue steadfast!'"

But, in the first place, is it certain that, had Swift surrendered himself, Harding, who was charged with another offence altogether, would be released? The certainty is all the other way; and Swift by surrendering himself, would have helped his printer no better than Sheridan helped the drunkard who appealed to him to lift him out of the gutter:—"I can't do that," hiccoughed Sheridan, himself far gone in his cups, "but I'll tell you what I'll do for you: I'll lie down beside you."

And, in the second place, as Swift reminds Harding in "Directions to the Printer" affixed to the "Letter to Lord Molesworth," the Dean had repeatedly cautioned the publisher to get before publishing—as Harding did—the assurance of the best legal advice that there was nothing incriminating in the "Letters."

But the lawyers, who advised Harding to this effect reckoned without Chief Justice Whitshed, whom Swift certainly had in his mind in this very "Letter to Lord Molesworth," when he recalls the judge "who, upon the criminal's appeal to the dreadful Day of Judgment, told him that he had incurred a *premunire* by appealing to a foreign jurisdiction." It appears to me that Swift did all that he could for Harding—and, indeed, all that could be done for him—by fortifping the Grand Jury against his Whitshed's browbeating. In a letter addressed to this Grand Jury, written, like the rest, with a kind of electric-light coldness, clearness, and penetrating intensity, Swift shows that the cause advocated in the incriminated Letter, was the cause of Ireland in general, and of the members of the Grand Jury—Irish merchants and shopkeepers—in particular, and winds up with a fable whose moral is never out of date in this country :—

"I will conclude all with a fable ascribed to Demosthenes. He had served the people of Athens with great fidelity in the station of an orator, when upon a certain occasion, apprehending to be delivered over to his enemies, he told the Athenians, his countrymen, the following story: 'Once upon a time the wolves desired a league with the sheep, upon this condition, that the cause of strife might be taken away, which was the shepherds and mastiffs. This being granted, the wolves without all fear, made havoc of the sheep.'"

This letter told, and told even more triumphantly than Swift could have expected. Not only did this Grand Jury resist Whitshed's browbeating so doggedly that the exasperated Chief Justice actually and arrogantly dissolved them; but its successor carried the war into the camp of the foe by making a presentment against the halfpence!

Swift triumphed, the halfpence were withdrawn, but it was, or at least it seemed, a Cadmean victory. The only lesson the "Drapier" controversy taught Walpole was to make Ireland a more absolutely and abjectly "dependent kingdom" than ever. Swift, says Sheridan, upon hearing that a great crowd had assembled to witness an eclipse, sent out a bellman to proclaim that "The eclipse had been postponed by the Dean's orders;" whereupon the crowd resignedly dispersed. The total eclipse of Irish freedom under the reign of Archbishop Hugh Boulter was quite as much out of the range and reach of the Dean's proclamations. Walpole had but loosened his hold for a moment of Ireland in order to get a better purchase and a tighter grip, and the hand which he used—sheathed in the glove of the viceroy of the day—was that of this Protestant Primate. Archbishop Hugh Boulter was a perfect impersonation of English Government, hard, strong, unsympathetic, arrogant, and, to borrow an image from Johnson, "narrow as the neck of a vinegar cruet." Such government is either selfish, or shortsighted—either that of a statesman who foresees that he is damming up an inevitable flood, but is concerned only to postpone it—*Après nous le déluge;* or that of a quack who really believes that to drive in a disease is to cure it. But whether a crime or a blunder, government of this kind necessarily defeats itself in the long run, and has soon or late to pay compound interest both in difficulties and in concessions. Yet through some defects in the National character—probably of sympathy and of magnanimity—England has never once in all our history made to Ireland an inevitable concession either seasonably or graciously.

CHAPTER X.

"A MODEST PROPOSAL."

HE outcry raised by the "colonists" against oppression of a kind immeasurably lighter than that they were themselves inflicting upon the native Irish, reminds one of Fag's complaining of an unprovoked push from young Absolute while himself severely belabouring the unoffending page. But the outcry itself was amply justified. Archbishop Boulter's idea, which he formulated explicitly and rigidly carried out, was to govern Ireland, not only for England and from England, but by and through Englishmen exclusively. His ideal was like that Swift attributes to Lord Sunderland:—"That all who have had the misfortune to be born in Ireland should be rendered incapable of holding any employment whatsoever above the degree

of constable." "All the great places must be filled by Englishmen," writes Boulter, "if we are to have quiet here." Accordingly every post of profit or importance is given to an Englishman untainted by any love, or care, or knowledge of Ireland, till Boulter can write, in 1729, "For five years the Government has been in English hands." Yet are the Irish-born English unconscionably discontented! "Many of our own original," he exclaims in perplexity at their perversity, "esteem us Englishmen as intruders!" I do not know how it is that in every country England has annexed and exploited natives will be found to regard them almost as much in the light of intruders as though they had been Russians, French, or Germans. But in this case, where the men cuckooed out of the nest were themselves of English origin, there is, I think, some explanation, or extenuation, at least, of the dissatisfaction which so perplexed Archbishop Boulter.

"Besides," writes Swift in his seventh 'Drapier's Letter,' "the prodigious profit which England receives by the transmittal thither of two-thirds of the revenues of this old kingdom, it has another mighty advantage, by making our country a receptacle wherein to disburden themselves of their supernumerary pretenders to office. Persons of second-rate merit in their own country, who, like birds of passage, most of them thrive and fatten here, and fly off when their credit and employments are it an end. So that Ireland may justly say, what Luther said of himself, 'POOR Ireland makes many rich!'"

One of the consequences of this wholesale importation of Englishmen was a yet more wholesale exportation—almost the only export trade allowed to us—of Irishmen to England. As the extinction of trade drove from the country such of the poor as could afford to get away from it, so the official boycotting of the upper class sent them also in shoals to England. In Ireland their Irish birth disqualified them for office only; but, for the rest, mattered as little as Hamlet's madness would have mattered in England, since "there the men were as mad as he." In England, however, the social discredit of their Irish birth could be made up for only by a lavish display of wealth, and this wealth was extorted from rack-rented tenants. Thus it came about that the Irish absentee landlord drew most from the country to which he returned least. Seeing, too, nothing of the frightful misery he caused, he had no remorse and was moved to no mitigation of it. Another of the consequences of fastening all these needy Englishmen on the body of Ireland—as the wealthy Buddhist transfers to the body of a poorer brother all the vermin which his creed forbids him to kill upon his own—was, that not only the whole of the bloated Irish Pension List, but the bulk of the official salaries of these English blood-suckers was spent in England. What arguments, asks Swift with biting sarcasm, can an Irish viceroy address now to an Irish Parliament, since not only all the offices, but all the reversions of the offices in his gift, have been made over to Englishmen who for the most part spend their emoluments in England?

"All considerable offices for life are here possessed by those to whom reversions were granted; and these have been generally followers of the chief governors, or persons who had interest in the Court of England. So the Lord Berkeley of Stratton holds that great office of Master of the Rolls; the Lord Palmerston is first Remembrancer, worth near £2,000 per annum. One Doddington, secretary to the Earl of Pembroke, begged the reversion of Clerk of the Pells, worth £2,500 a year, which he now enjoys by the death of Lord Newtown. Mr. Southwell is Secretary of State, and the Earl of Burlington Lord High Treasurer of Ireland by inheritance. These are only a few among many others which I have been told of, but cannot remember. Nay, the reversion of several employments, during pleasure, is granted the same way. This, among many others, is a circumstance whereby the kingdom of Ireland is distinguished from all other nations upon earth, and makes it so difficult an affair to get into a civil employ, that Mr. Addison was forced to purchase an old obscure place, called Keeper of the Records in Bermingham's Tower, of £10 a year, and to get a salary of £400 annexed to it, though all the records there are not worth half-a-crown either for curiosity or use. And we lately saw a favourite Secretary descend to be Master of the Revels, which by his credit and extortion he has made pretty considerable. I say nothing of the Under-Treasurership, worth about £9,000 a year, nor of the commissioners of the revenue, four of whom generally live in England, for I think none of these are granted in reversion. But the jest is, that I have known, upon occasion, some of these absent officers as keen against the interest of Ireland, as if they had never been indebted to her for a single groat."

The country, being bled thus at every vein, with nothing to restore its strength, resembled one of those tillage farms to which Swift frequently refers, cropped by each succeeding short-leased tenant, whose interest it was to extract everything and return nothing to the exhausted soil.

It is the poor of a country so crushed to earth that, being at the bottom, have the accumulated load of its misery to bear; and the sufferings of the Irish poor at this period were frightful. Swift did what he could at much risk, as we have seen, and with some effect, in his "Proposal for the Universal Use of Irish Manufacture," to provide the starving Irish artizans with bread, in place of that which mere English envy had snatched from them. Indeed, he never lost sight of this object, or allowed his friends or dependents to lose sight of it. Giving a guinea to a friend's maid-servant, he charged her to buy with it a gown of Irish stuff. Finding her, however, on his next visit still in her old gown, he took her to task for misapplying his vail. She hurried from the room without a word, to return presently with her apron filled with books. "Here, please your reverence, is the Irish stuff I have bought with your guinea, and better was never manufactured!" They were Swift's works. It would be hard to say whether the compliment or the guinea was better deserved. The story illustrates Swift's zeal in the cause of Irish trade, its appreciation, and its effect. Ireland's staple industry—agriculture—however was, and might well be, his despair. Not the taxation of the country alone, and its numberless sinecure salaries and pensions were spent in England, but also the bulk of its rack-rents. Through these and other causes the agricultural districts of the country were reduced chronically almost to the condition to which they were brought temporarily in the year of the great famine.

"At least five children in six who are born," writes Swift in his 'Maxims Controlled in Ireland,' "lie a dead weight upon us for want of employment. And a very skilful computer assured me that above one half of the souls in this kingdom supported themselves by begging and thievery; two-thirds whereof would be able to get their bread in any other country upon earth. Trade is the only incitement to labour; where that fails, the poorer native must either beg, steal, or starve, or be forced to quit his country. . . . I confess myself to be touched with very sensible pleasure, when I hear of a mortality in any country parish or village, where the wretches are forced to pay for a filthy cabin, and two ridges of potatoes, treble their worth; brought up to steal or beg for want of work; to whom death would be the best thing to be wished for on account both of themselves and of the public."

According to all contemporary accounts, the bulk of the population were degraded to the level of the beasts of the field in every particular but this—that it was no one's interest to feed, herd, or tend them. Having to beg, steal, or starve, they did one or other of the three, according to circumstances, and were, as Swift, suggests, happiest when their lot was the last. Their moral degradation, too, was as deep as their physical—so deep that even the virtue of chastity, which, to-day, seems an ineradicable Irish instinct, was uprooted. Girls allowed themselves to be debauched solely in order that they might excite compassion by posing as widows with babes at the breast; while, herding as they did like brutes together, incest and adultery were as common among these organized bands of beggars as they are uncommon, I might almost say unknown, among the Irish peasants of to-day.

Such was the frightful state of the country which provoked that terrible paper—the most terrible, I suppose, that ever was written—"A Modest Proposal." "*Guardati da aceto di vin dolce,*" says the Italian proverb, and the death cold and white ferocity of the "Modest Proposal" was a characteristically Swiftian expression of pity in despair. The paper, in truth, is the literary analogue of the kind of despairing pity which makes a mother, mad with misery, drown her child to save it from a life of horror. Those who can see in the act of such a mother insane hate, and not insane love, of her child, are as wise and sympathetic as those who can see in "A Modest Proposal" callous insensibility to the suffering of which it shows a maddened and despairing sensitiveness.

The keynote of the paper is, in fact, that passage towards its close, in which Swift protests that he makes this proposal only because all the other remedies for the maddening miseries of the country which he has been urging and urging for years, have been pressed upon it and its rulers in vain:—

"I can think of no one objection that will possibly be raised against this proposal, unless it should be urged that the number of the people will be thereby much lessened in the kingdom. This I freely own, and it was, indeed, one principal design in offering it to the world. I desire the reader will observe that I calculate my remedy for this one individual kingdom of Ireland, and for no other that ever was, is, or, I think, ever can be upon earth. Therefore let no man talk to me of other expedients—of taxing our absentees at five shillings a pound—of using neither clothes, nor household furniture, except what is our own growth and manufacture—of utterly rejecting the materials and instruments that promote foreign luxury—of curing the expensiveness of pride, vanity, idleness and gaming in our women—of introducing a vein of parsimony, prudence, and temperance—of learning to love our country, in the want of which we differ even from Laplanders and the inhabitants of Topinambo—of quitting our animosities and factions, nor acting any longer like the Jews, who were murdering one another at the very moment their city was taken—of being a little cautious not to sell our country and conscience for nothing—of teaching landlords to have at least one degree of mercy towards their tenants—lastly, of putting a spirit of honesty, industry, and skill into our shop-keepers, who, if a resolution could now be taken to buy only our native goods, would immediately unite to cheat and exact upon us in the price, the measure and the goodness, nor could ever yet be brought to make one fair proposal of just dealing, though often and earnestly invited to it. Therefore, I repeat, let no man talk to me of these and the like expedients, till he has at least some glimpse of hope that there will be ever some hearty and sincere attempt to put them in practice. But as to myself, having been wearied out for years with offering vain, idle, visionary thoughts, and at length utterly despairing of success, I fortunately fell upon this proposal; which, as it is wholly new, so it has something solid and real, of no expense and little trouble, full in our own power, and whereby we can incur no danger of disobliging England."

England would not put her usual veto upon the scheme—(to use up for food the superfluous children of the poor)—for two reasons; first, because there would be no interference with her markets, and, secondly, because she would herself willingly eat up the entire Irish nation without salt.

"For the kind of commodity will not bear exportation, the flesh being of too tender a consistence to admit a long continuance in salt; although, perhaps, I could name a country which would be glad to eat up our whole nation without it."

The paper, then, was the sardonic expression of a frenzy of despair at the failure of all his efforts to move England to help Ireland, or Ireland to help herself. It was written at the same date and in the same spirit of that letter to Bolingbroke, in which Swift groans that he sees nothing before him but to "die here in a rage, like a poisoned rat in a hole." The yoke that he had a little lightened and loosened was pressed down again more remorselessly than ever by Walpole and Boulter upon the necks of the people till the last state of the country was worse than the first. How anyone can read the "Modest Proposal," and doubt that pity, and not pitilessness, was its inspiration, I cannot imagine. What an intensity of pity, soured by despair inspires the irony of such passages as this?—

"Some persons of a desponding spirit are in great concern about that vast number of poor people who are aged, diseased, and maimed, and I have been desired to employ my thoughts what course may be taken to ease the nation of so grievous an incumbrance. But I am not in the least pain upon that matter, because it is very well known that they are every day dying and rotting by cold and famine, and filth and vermin, as fast as can be reasonably expected. And, as to the young labourers, they are now in almost as hopeful a condition. They cannot get work, and consequently pine away for want of nourishment to a degree that if at any time they are accidentally hired to common labour, they have not strength to perform it; and thus the country and themselves are happily delivered from the evil to come."

On the other hand, it must be admitted that all the details of the horrid project are described with the zest and minuteness of a dissecting-room demonstrator, to whom the mangled corpse on the table is only as a figure in Euclid. As, however, in some diseases, everything turns to acid in the system, so everything in Swift turned to that *sæva indignatio*, which, like the vulture of Prometheus, tore for ever at his heart. He had, besides, a morbid, and, as it seems to me, an insane taste for the horrible or the nasty details of any subject of his scorn. His revolting picture of human nature, for instance, in his "Voyage to the Houyhnhnms," reminds you of nothing so much as a guide in Paris, who showed you only the sewers. The sewers, no doubt, are there, and are an essential feature of the city, but they are not Paris. The details of his ghoulish

"Modest Proposal" have a similar fascination for him, but the project itself, like the picture of human nature in the "Voyage to the Houyhnhnms," was inspired by *sæva indignatio*, by an insupportable sense of the miseries of the poor Irish taking the usual turn in such a nature as Swift's of fell hate and scorn of their oppressors. For the "Modest Proposal" is and was meant to be, the most terrible arraignment of a Government that ever was penned.

CHAPTER XI.

"ON DOING GOOD."

E associate a divine with a pulpit, and a dean with a theological treatise, but Swift's Rabelaisian theological treatise, *A Tale of a Tub*, characteristically associates the pulpit with the stroller's stage and the gallows—"three wooden machines for the use of those orators who desire to talk much without interruption." Neither this association, nor the treatise in which it occurs, would lead you to look for effective pulpit oratory from the Dean of St. Patrick's; yet he preached at least one sermon which we have high authority for considering the best of its kind ever delivered.

"Swift's pieces relating to Ireland," says Edmund Burke, "are those of a public nature, in which the Dean appears, as usual, in the best light, because they do honour to his heart as well as his head, furnishing some additional proofs, that, though he was very free in his abuse of the inhabitants of that country, as well natives as foreigners, he had their interest sincerely at heart, and perfectly understood it. His sermon on doing good, though peculiarly adapted to Ireland, and Wood's design upon it, contains perhaps the best motives to patriotism that was ever delivered within so small a compass."

It is certainly an excellent specimen of an eighteenth century Anglican sermon—a prosaic species. The Anglican divines of this century seemed to regard God as a kind of almighty Walpole, and man at his best as of the sordid sort of stuff of which small shopkeepers are supposed to be made—amenable only to the fear of loss and punishment, or to the hope of gain and reward. Perhaps it was a more practical religion than most of the high-pressure piety of to-day, which seems to let all the steam off through the safety-valve or the whistle till there is none to turn on to the wheels; but it was so little spiritual as to remind you of the benighted disciples at Ephesus who "had not so much as heard whether there be any Holy Ghost."

To this species of moral essay belongs Swift's discourse "On Doing Good," preached from the text, "As we have therefore opportunity, let us do good unto all men." As it contains; according to Burke, "the best motives to patriotism that was ever delivered within so small a compass," and as the kind of practical patriotism it preaches is not that most in vogue or in action to-day in our country, I shall proceed to quote from it extensively. In opening it, I think Swift must have had in his mind Bacon's distinction:

"Beware how in making the portraiture, thou breakest the pattern; for Divinity maketh the love of ourselves the pattern, the love of our neighbours the portraiture."

Swift starts with the same distinction:

"Nature directs every one of us, and God permits us, to consult our own private good before the private good of any other person whatsoever. We are, indeed, commanded to love our neighbour as ourselves, but not as well as ourselves. The love we have for ourselves is to be the pattern of that love we ought to have toward our neighbour; but as the copy doth not equal the original, so my neighbour cannot think it hard if I prefer myself, who am the original, before him, who is only the copy. Thus, if any matter equally concern the life, the reputation, the profit of my neighbour and my own, the law of nature, which is the law of God obligeth me to take care of myself first, and afterward of him. And this I need not be at much pains in persuading you, for the want of self-love with regard to things of this world, is not among the faults of mankind. But then, on the other side, if, by a small hurt and loss to myself, I can procure a great good to my neighbour, in that case his interest is to be preferred.

For example, if I can be sure of saving his life without great danger to my own; if I can preserve him from being undone without ruining myself; or recover his reputation without blasting mine—all this I am obliged to do, and, if I sincerely perform it, I do then obey the command of God in loving my neighbour as myself. But, besides this love we owe to every man in his particular capacity, under the title of our neighbour, there is yet a duty of a more large extensive nature incumbent on us—our love to our neighbour in his public capacity, as he is a member of that great body, the Commonwealth, under the same Government with ourselves—and this is usually called love of the public, and is a duty to which we are more strictly obliged than even that of loving ourselves, because therein ourselves are also contained —as well as all our neighbours—in one great body. The love of the public, or of the Commonwealth, or love of our country, was in ancient times properly known by the name of virtue, because it was the greatest of all virtues, and was supposed to contain all virtues in it; and many great examples of this virtue are left us on record, scarcely to be believed, or even conceived, in such a base, corrupted, wicked age as this we live in. In those times it was common for men to sacrifice their lives for the good of their country, although they had neither hope nor belief of future rewards; whereas, in our days, very few make the least scruple of sacrificing a whole nation, as well as their own souls, for a little present gain—which often hath been known to end in their own ruin in this world, as it certainly must in that to come. Have we not seen men for the sake of some petty employment give up the very natural rights and liberties of their country, and of mankind, in the ruin of which themselves must at last be involved? Are not these corruptions gotten among the meanest of our people, who for a piece of money will give their votes at a venture for the disposal of their own lives and fortunes, without considering whether it be to those who are most likely to betray or defend them? But, if I were to produce only one instance of a hundred wherein we fail in this duty of loving our country it would be an endless labour, and therefore I shall not attempt it."

Swift then, addressing, of course, only his co-colonists and co-religionists in St. Patrick's Cathedral, proceeds to distinguish between loyalty and patriotism, as though there was a possibility of their being confounded in Ireland. To us to-day in Ireland the two sentiments seem nearly related only in Lady Teazle's sense —"So near a kin that they can never be united"—for Irish loyalty and Irish patriotism are almost invariably found to be in inverse proportion to each other.

"But here I would not be misunderstood. By the love of our country, I do not mean loyalty to our king, for that is a duty of another nature, and a man may be very loyal, in the common sense of the word, without one grain of public good in his heart. Witness this very kingdom we live in. I verily believe, that since the beginning of the world, no nation upon earth ever showed (all circumstances considered) such high constant marks of loyalty in all their actions and behaviour as we have done; and, at the same time, no people ever appeared more utterly void of what is called public spirit. When I say the people, I mean the bulk or mass of the people, for I have nothing to do with those in power. Therefore, I shall think my time not ill-spent if

I can persuade most or all of you who hear me, to show the love you have for your country by endeavouring in your several situations to do all the public good you can. For I am certainly persuaded that all our misfortunes arise from no other original cause than that general disregard among us to the public welfare."

It must, however, be remembered that the excess of loyalty and defect in public spirit of this class then were incomparably more despicable and inexcusable than they are now. Now the Queen is to this class the symbol of ascendency, and loyalty is but its protest against a claim (become formidable) of the bulk of the people to political equality or even supremacy. But in Swift's day the bulk of the people were, in his own words, "as inconsiderable in point of power as the women and children;" while the oppression against which he was protesting crushed the colonists specially. To them, therefore, loyalty meant, not the acknowledgment of a dog of the support of his master at his back while worrying its prey, but a spaniel-like licking of the foot of the master that spurned it. Again, while to-day patriotism and public spirit might plausibly be denounced by the ascendency party as meaning the consideration exclusively of the interests of the bulk of the people; in Swift's day they meant consideration of its own interests exclusively. Yet he says, and says truly, that since the beginning of the world no nation ever showed such an excess of loyalty and such a lack of public spirit and patriotism.

In the hope of supplying this lack Swift proceeds to show three things:—First, that there are few people so weak or obscure as not to have it sometimes in their power to be useful to the public. Secondly, that it is often in the power of the most obscure and weak of mankind to do mischief to the public. And, lastly, that all wilful injuries done to the public are aggravated sins in the sight of God. Having given historical instances of the great good or great ill that can be done to the public by the weak or the obscure he passes on to urge that patriotism should ever be on the alert.

"Hence it clearly follows how necessary the love of our country, or a public spirit is in every particular man, since the wicked have so many opportunities of doing public mischief. Every man is upon his guard for his private advantage; but where the public is concerned, he is apt to be negligent, considering himself as only one among two or three millions, among whom the loss is equally shared, and thus, he thinks, he can be no great sufferer. Meanwhile the trader, the farmer, and the shop-keeper complain of the hardness and deadness of the times, and wonder whence it comes, while it is in a great measure owing to their own folly, for want of that love of their country, and public spirit and firm union among themselves, which are so necessary to the prosperity of every nation. . . . Thus, we see the public is many times, as it were, at the mercy of the meanest instrument who can be wicked enough to watch opportunities of doing it mischief upon the principles of avarice or malice, which I am afraid are deeply rooted in too many breasts, and against which there can be no defence but a firm resolution in all honest men to be closely united and active in showing their love to their country, by preferring the public interest to their private advantage. If a passenger in a great storm at sea should hide his goods that they might not be thrown overboard to lighten the ship, what would be the consequence? The ship is cast away, and he loses his life and goods together."

Finally Swift urges arguments appropriate to the sacred place and day and service—that government is from God, confusion from the devil, and that the man who would take the government out of God's hands to put it into those of the devil—to the great injury of the Commonwealth—commits a greater crime than any, how heinous soever, committed against a private person. Besides, it is a kind of impiety in itself to be unpatriotic.

"All offences against our country have this aggravation—that they are ungrateful and unnatural. It is to our country we owe those laws which protect us in our lives, liberties, our properties, and our religion. Our country produced us into the world, and continues to nourish us, so that it is usually called our mother, and there have been examples of great magistrates who have put their own children to death for endeavouring to betray their country, as if they had attempted the life of their natural parent."

This sermon, I allow, reads a little like the prospectus of a company which offers clear and even substantial profit to *bona fide* investors. There is a balance-sheet of profit and loss, and a calculation as clear and cold and logical as that of a rule-of-three sum, which makes as little of an appeal to the feelings as any such arithmetical demonstration. This, however, was the style of the Anglican sermons of the day, and Swift's discourse is, if low in its flight, at least direct, and strong, and, above all, well aimed. As he never drew a bow at a venture, he made, we may be sure, the kind of appeal which would weigh most with his audience. From the character of this appeal alone it would be safe to infer the character of the congregation to whom it was addressed—not to the Presbyterians of the North, who would need more pious unction, nor to the Catholics and Celts, who would need more sentiment and rhetoric—but to the cold and matter-of-fact Anglicans, to whom "dry light is best." And these few thousand Anglicans were to Swift "the nation," whose battle alone—politically—he was roused to fight.

CHAPTER XII.

"THE STORY OF THE INJURED LADY."

THE author of *Gulliver's Travels* was not likely to leave untried as an instrument of political instruction the parable—naturally the most primitive, popular and telling of all appeals to the unsophisticated understanding.

"Where truth in closest words shall fail,
   There truth embodied in a tale
Shall enter in at lowly doors.

"Which he may read that binds the sheaf,
   Or builds the house, or digs the grave,
   And those wild eyes that watch the wave
In roarings round the coral reef."

Such parables of the wrongs of Ireland and of their

remedies Swift gives us in "The Story of the Injured Lady," and in the "Answer to the Injured Lady," from which an eminent living statesman assures us he derived no little instruction in his youth. The injured Lady is Ireland; her rival, is Scotland; the false lover, who has as grossly ill-used her as he has favoured her rival, is England. Such an ill-used lady in life would feel infinitely more furious with the rival, for whom she was neglected, than with the faithless swain who neglected her, and here Swift rejoices in being true to life. His detestation of the Scotch, which finds such ferocious expression in his annotations of Burnet.—"Most damnable Scots," "Scotch hell-hounds," etc.—had a more personal origin than his theological horror of Presbyterianism. Probably, indeed, his theological horror of Presbyterianism arose originally from his personal grudge against the sect and side which caused in the Civil War the ruin of his family and the exile to Ireland of his father. Whatever may have been its origin, the intense bitterness of his prejudice against the Scotch and their creed so jaundiced his politics as to affect his career at its chief crisis; since his alienation from the Whigs was quite as much due to their desire and design of abolishing the Test Act in Ireland, as to their neglect of his Church's interests and of his own.

The Injured Lady, therefore, reviles her rival with a lifelike virrulence before proceeding to instance all the acts of cruelty and oppression committed by her estranged lover. I need not say that the Ireland represented by the Injured Lady is the little Church-of-England colony in that country to the exclusion of both Catholics and Presbyterians, who figure in the parable as "ignorant, illiterate" dependents; that the steward is the king, and the under-steward the viceroy:—

"Some years ago this gentleman, taking a fancy either to my person or fortune, made his addresses to me, which, being then young and foolish, I readily admitted. When he had once got possession, he began to play the usual part of a too fortunate lover, affecting on all occasions to show his authority, and to act like a conquerer. First, he found fault with the government of my family, which, I grant was none of the best, consisting of ignorant, illiterate persons, for at that time I knew but little of the world. In compliance to him, therefore, I agreed to fall into his ways and methods of living; I have liberty to employ an under-steward who should receive his directions. My lover proceeded farther, turned away several old servants and tenants, and supplying me with others from his own house. These grew so domineering and unreasonable that there was no quiet, and I heard of nothing but perpetual quarrels, which, although I could not possibly help, yet my lover laid all the blame and punishment upon me, and upon every falling out still turned away more of my people, and supplied me in their stead with a number of fellows and dependents of his own, whom he had no other way to provide for. Overcome by love and to avoid noise and contention, I yielded to all his usurpations, and, finding it in vain to resist, I thought it my best policy to make my court to my new servants, and draw them to my interests; I fed them from my own table with the best I had, put my new tenants on the best parts of my land, and treated them all so kindly that they began to love me as well as their master. In process of time, all my old servants were gone, and I had not a creature about me, nor above one or two tenants, but what were of his choosing; yet I had the good luck by gentle usage to bring over the greatest part of them to my side. When my lover observed this, he began to alter his language, and to those who enquired about me he would answer that I was an old dependent of his family, whom he had placed on some concerns of his own, and he began to use me accordingly, neglecting by degrees all common civility in his behaviour. I shall never forget the speech he made me one morning which he delivered with all the gravity in the world. He put me in mind of the vast obligations I lay under to him in sending me so many of his people for my own good, and to teach me manners; that it had cost him ten times more than I was worth to maintain me; that it had been much better for him if I had been burnt, or sunk to the bottom of the sea; that it was reasonable I should strain myself as far as I was able to reimburse him some of his charges; that from henceforward he expected his word should be law to me in all things; that I must maintain a parish watch against thieves and robbers, and give salaries to an overseer, a constable, and others of his own choosing, whom he would send from time to time to be spies upon me; that to enable me the better in supporting these expenses, my tenants should be obliged to carry all their goods across the river to his own town-market, and pay toll on both sides, and then sell them at half value. But because we were a nasty sort of people, and that he could not endure to touch anything we had a hand in, and, likewise, because he wanted work to employ his own folks, therefore we must send all our goods to his market just in their naturals—the milk immediately from the cow, without making into cheese or butter; the corn in the ear, the grass as it was mowed, the wool as it comes from the sheep's back, and bring the fruit upon the branch, that he might not be obliged to eat it out of our filthy hands. That, if a tenant carried but a piece of bread and cheese to eat by the way, or an inch of worsted to mend his stockings, he should forfeit his whole parcel. And because a parcel of rogues usually plied on the river between us, who often robbed my tenants of their goods and boats, he ordered a waterman of his own to guard them, whose manner was to be out of the way till the poor wretches were plundered, then to overtake the thieves and sieze all as lawful prize to his master and himself. It would be endless to repeat a hundred other hardships he has put upon me, but it is a general rule that whenever he imagines the smallest advantage will redound to one of his footboys by any new oppression of me and my whole family and estate, he never disputeth it a moment. All this has rendered me so very insignificant and contemptible at home, that some servants to whom I pay the greatest wages and many tenants, who have the most beneficial leases, are gone over to live with him, yet I am bound to continue their wages and to pay their rents, by which means one-third of my income is spent on his estate, and above another third by his tolls and markets, and my poor tenants are so sunk and impoverished that, instead of maintaining me suitably to my quality, they can hardly find me clothes to keep me warm, or provide the common necessaries of life for themselves. . . . I am sure I never sought this alliance, and you can bear me witness that I might have had other matches; nay, if I were lightly disposed, I could still, perhaps, have offers that some who hold their heads higher would be glad to accept. But, alas! I never had any such wicked thought. All I now desire is only to enjoy a little quiet, to be free from the persecutions of this unreasonable man, and that he will let me manage my own little fortune to the best advantage, for which I will undertake to pay him a considerable pension every year—much more considerable than what he now gets from his oppressions; for he must needs find himself a loser at last, when he has drained me and my tenants so dry, that we shall not have a penny for him or ourselves. There is one imposition of his I had almost forgot, which I think insufferable, and will appeal to you or any reasonable person whether it is or not. I told you before that by an old compact we agreed to have the same steward, at which time I consented likewise to regulate my family and estate by the same methods with him, which he then showed me written down in form, and I approved of. Now, the turn he thinks fit to give this compact of ours is very extraordinary, for he pretends that whatever orders he shall think fit to prescribe for the future in his family, he may, if he will, compel mine to observe them without asking my advice or hearing my reasons. So that I must not make a lease without his consent, or give any directions for the well-governing of my family but what he countermands whenever he pleases. This leaves me at such confusion and uncertainty that my servants know not when to obey me, and my tenants, although many of them be very well inclined, seem quite at a loss. But I am too tedious upon this melancholy subject, which, however, I hope you will forgive, since the happiness of my whole life depends upon it. I desire you will think awhile, and give your best advice what measures I shall take with prudence, justice, courage and honour, to protect my liberty and fortune against the hardships and severities I lie under from that unkind, inconstant man."

Here is the letter with the omission of the tart references to Scotland, and it fairly summarises Swift's idea, not only of the relations of Ireland to England, but of the mutual relations of the different races and religions in Ireland. The English colony was the Injured Lady; the Government officials were her servants; the landlords, her tenants; the tenants and labourers her dependents.

What position is more unhappy, helpless and hopeless than that of a woman wholly in the power of a man to whom she has surrendered everything, and who is scorned by him for that very surrender? He hates her, because he has injured her; despises her for her abject submission to his injuries; mortifies her for the mere pleasure of mortifying her, and opposes her wishes only because they are her's.

Such precisely was the bearing of England towards the Ireland of that day which was of any political account. Why? Because the Ireland then of any political account was weak as a woman. The Church-of-England garrison, a mere handful compared with the Presbyterian Scotch of the North and the Irish Catholics of the South and West, had to look to England from moment to moment for the maintenance of their exclusive privileges and their supreme position; and England exacted from their helpless dependence the uttermost farthing in payment of this indispensable support.

The sixth-form schoolboy, if he bullies his fag infernally, backs up the wretched creature in his bullying in turn the boys of his own form, and by making him a tyrant rewards him for being a slave. The tyranny of the ascendency, as Swift elsewhere contended, was the direct product of the tyranny of England, while it in turn produced a third the most degrading and grinding of all—the tyranny of the agent.

"All this has rendered me so very insignificant and contemptible at home," complains the Injured Lady, "that some servants to whom I pay the greatest wages, and many tenants who have the most beneficial leases, are gone over to live with him, yet I am bound to continue their wages and to pay their rents; by which means one-third of my income is spent on his estate, and above another third by his tolls and markets."

The landlords and Government officials fled the ruined country, precipitating its ruin by their flight, and the deputies they appointed whipped the people with scorpions. The smaller the tyrant, the greater the tyranny naturally, since a man's sole claim to importance must be kept by him always in evidence for his own and others' assurance of his consequence. Thus there was no tyranny so galling and continual as that of these deputy tyrants, who, like the cur-dog in "King Lear," denied the poor even an approach and appeal to their masters.

Drained dry through these three tyrannies—by pensions, duties, rents and taxes—the country had nearly come to the pass of bankruptcy:

"He must needs find himself a loser at last, when he has drained me and my tenants so dry that we shall not have a penny for him or ourselves."

At this point the lover becomes the injured person, and upbraids the lady he had beggared with her beggary:

"I shall never forget the speech he made me one morning, which he delivered with all the gravity in the world. He put me in mind of the vast obligations I lay under to him in sending me so many of his people for my own good, and to teach me manners; that it had cost him ten times more than I was worth to maintain me; that it had been much better for him if I had been burnt, or sunk to the bottom of the sea; that it was reasonable I should strain myself as far as I was able to reimburse him of some of his charges."

The wish, which we have since heard so often—that

Ireland were sunk in the Atlantic—must have been then more fervent and frequent, since the instinct of a pirate is to scuttle the ship he has plundered. As, however, Ireland was not to be so disposed of, she was towed helplessly in the track of her captor, a dismantled hulk.

"There is one imposition of his I had almost forgot, which I think insufferable, and will appeal to you or to any reasonable person whether it be so or not. I told you before that by an old compact we agreed to have the same steward, at which time I consented likewise to regulate my family and estate by the same method with him, which he then showed me written down in form, and I approved of. Now, the turn he thinks fit to give this compact of ours is very extraordinary; for he pretends that whatever orders he shall think fit to prescribe for the future in his family, he may, if he will, compel mine to observe them without asking my advice, or hearing my reasons."

Such was the case put by the Injured Lady to her friend, who replies (omitting again the biting references to Scotland, which take up two-thirds of the brief letter) with the following sound advice:

"I know the matters of fact as you relate them are true, and fairly represented. My advice, therefore, is this: Get your tenants together as soon as you conveniently can, and make them agree to the following resolutions:—

"First, that your family and servants have no dependence upon the said gentlemen farther than by the old agreement, which obliges you to have the same steward, and to regulate your households by such methods as you should both agree to.

"Secondly, that you will not carry your goods to the market of his town, unless you please, nor be hindered from carrying them anywhere else.

"Thirdly, that the servants you pay wages to shall live at home, or forfeit their places.

"Fourthly, that whatever lease you make to a tenant, it shall not be in his power to break it.

"If he will agree to these articles, I advise you to contribute as largely as you can to all charges of parish and county. I can assure you several of the gentlemen's ablest tenants and servants are against his severe usage of you, and would be glad of an occasion to convince the rest of their error, if you will not be wanting to yourself."

"If you will not be wanting to yourself." It all lies, and will always lie in that. "Every country," says Montesquieu, "gets the government it deserves," and to complain continually of slavery is to confess continual unworthiness of freedom. It would be hardly too much to say that once at least in each generation the opportunity of freedom is given, and the nation that refuses the great offer deserves the fate assigned by Dante to the refusal—*Che fece per viltate gran rifiuto.* The people which sits supinely waiting to be set free may be set free, but cannot be made freemen, or long retain freedom, because freedom is not a dole to be accepted, but a challenge-shield to be won and to be held against all comers. Ireland, however, has had against her not only the odds, to use Swift's figure, of "eleven men armed against a single man in his shirt," and of a kingdom divided against itself, but also, as I shall now proceed to show, of centuries of such sharp slavery as pierced to the soul.

CHAPTER XIII.

MORAL EFFECTS OF OPPRESSION.

So far I have tried to give adequate specimens of Swift's protests against the oppression, political, commercial and agricultural, of the Ireland of his day; but of another protest he made with equal force and frequency, and perhaps equal effect, I have said little. He saw, as we can see still to-day, that the deadliest effects of continued oppression are not material, but moral—the impoverishment of the spirit of a people, and not the mere impoverishment of their resources. The hackneyed quotation:—

"Who steals my purse steals trash; 'tis something,
    nothing,
'Twas mine, 'tis his, and has been slave to thousands;
But he that filches from me my good name
Robs me of that which not enriches him,
And makes me poor, indeed,"

extravagantly overrates "the bubble reputation;" since

a man can be made poor indeed only by the loss, not of his purse or of his good name, but of his self-respect Of this long continued oppression robs a people, and its loss outweighs and also outlasts all the other effects of tyranny. Upon the uplifting of such oppression a people does not spring up erect at once, like grass from under a fairy foot-fall, but lies, as I have sometimes seen a fallen horse lie, even after not only its crushing load, but its very harness has been lifted off it. Its vain efforts to gain its feet under the load, have so cowed its spirit that it cannot for some time after its removal be persuaded to renew them. No one will say that Ireland has even yet recovered the spring of its spirit which centuries of oppression and repression have bowed. It would, in truth, be surprising if some of the characteristics Swift notes as those of a long-enslaved people did not linger still amongst us to-day; and if, therefore, his reproofs and exhortations had for us only an historic interest.

What, then, were these moral results of oppression noted by Swift? I think all, or almost all, might be classed under the general head of childishness—a childish lack of initiative, of staying power and perseverance, and of foresight, forethought and providence. But the kind of childishness which first and most of all strikes Swift is that of a cowed and cowering schoolboy.

"My Lord," he writes in a letter to Archbishop King, concerning the weavers, "the Corporation of weavers in the woollen manufacture, who have so often attended your Grace and called upon me with their schemes and proposals, were with me on Thursday last, when he who spoke for the rest and in the name of his absent brethren, said:—'It was the opinion of the whole body that if somewhat was written at this time by an able hand to persuade the people of this kingdom to wear their own woollen manufactures, it might be of good use to the nation in general, and preserve many hundreds of the trade from starving.' To which I answered: 'That it was hard for any man of common spirit to turn his thoughts to such speculations without discovering a resentment which people are too delicate to bear.' For I will not deny to your Grace that I cannot reflect on the singular condition of this country, different from all others upon the face of the earth, without some emotion, and without often examining as I pass the streets whether those animals which come in my way with two legs and human faces, clad and erect, be of the same species with what I have seen very like in England as to the outward shape, but differing in their notions, natures, and intellectuals, more than any two kinds of brutes in the forest; which any man of common prudence would immediately discover by persuading them to define what they meant by law, liberty, property, courage, reason, loyalty or religion. One thing, my lord, I am very confident of—that if God Almighty for our sins would most justly send us a pestilence, whoever should dare to discover his grief in public for such a visitation, would certainly be censured for disaffection to the Government. For I solemnly profess that I do not know one calamity we have undergone these many years, which any man whose opinions were not in fashion, dared to lament, without being openly charged with that imputation. And this is the harder because, though a mother when she has corrected her child, may sometimes force it to kiss the rod, yet she will never give that power to the foot-boy or the scullion."

"A people long used to hardships," he writes elsewhere, "lose by degrees the very notions of liberty. They look upon themselves as creatures at mercy, and that all impositions laid on them by a stronger hand are, in the phrase of the report, legal and obligatory. Hence proceed that poverty and lowness of spirit to which a kingdom may be subject as well as a particular person. And when Esau came fainting from the field at the point to die, it is no wonder that he sold his birthright for a mess of pottage."

Poverty of spirit, like poverty of blood, comes from long keeping on low diet; and poverty, whether of spirit or of blood, in its turn produces other disorders. The vice of lying, for instance, comes of abjectness of spirit. "Montaigne prettily saith," writes Bacon, forgetting, by the way, that Montaigne was but quoting from Lysander, "Montaigne prettily saith, when he enquired the reason why the word of the 'lie' should be such a disgrace, and such an odious charge?" Saith he, "If it be well weighed, to say that a man lieth is as much as to say that he is brave toward God and a coward towards men. For a lie faces God, but shrinks from man."

Thieving, again, which with lying, is frequently denounced by Swift as distinctively and ineradicably the vice of the Irish poor, is the natural outcome of poverty both of condition and of spirit. Who, again, could severely blame the Irish farmer for the childish and even savage short-sightedness of his improvidence.

"It was, indeed," writes Swift, "the shameful practice of too many Irish farmers to wear out their ground with ploughing; while, either through poverty, laziness, or ignorance, they neither took care to measure it as they ought, nor gave time to any part of the land to recover itself. And, when their leases were near expiring, being assured that their landlords would not renew, they ploughed even the meadows, and made such havoc that their landlords were considerable sufferers by it. This gave rise to that abominable race of graziers, who, upon expiration of the farmers' leases, were ready to engross great quantities of land, and the gentlemen, having been often before ill paid, and their land worn out of heart, were too easily tempted, when a rich grazier made an offer to take all their land, and give them security for payment. Thus a vast tract of land, where twenty or thirty farmers lived, together with their cottagers and labourers in their several cabins, became all desolate and easily managed by one or two herdsmen and their boys; whereby the master grazier with little trouble seized to himself the livelihood of a hundred people. It must be confessed that the farmers were justly punished for their knavery, brutality and folly. But neither are the squires and landlords to be excused, for to them is owing the depopulating of the country, the vast numbers of beggars, and the ruin of those few sorry improvements we had."

Elsewhere, however, Swift suggests other reasons

than "knavery, brutality and folly" for this improvidence of the farmer :—

"The case in Ireland is yet somewhat worse; for the absentees of great estates, who, if they lived at home, would have many rich retainers in their neighbourhoods, have learned to rack their lands and shorten their leases, as much as any residing squire."

Why should farmers—not in any country a magnanimous race—sacrifice a present advantage to themselves to the future advantage of exterminating landlords? A like childish lack of initiative, of providence and of perseverance in the Irish artizan shopkeeper, and even manufacturer and merchant might fairly be traced to a like uncertainty of the tenure of their trade.

"The corporation of weavers in woollen and silk, who have so frequently offered proposals both to your Grace and to me, are the hottest and coldest generation of men that I have known. About a month ago they attended your Grace when I had the honour to be with you, and designed me the same favour. They desired you would recommend to your clergy to wear gowns of Irish stuffs which might probably spread the example among all their brethren in the kingdom, and perhaps among the lawyers and gentlemen of the University, and among the citizens of those corporations who appear in gowns on solemn occasions. I then mentioned a kind of stuff, not above eightpence a yard, which I heard had been contrived by some of the trade and was very convenient, I desired they would prepare some of that, or any sort of black stuff, on a certain day, when your Grace would appoint as many clergymen as could readily be found to meet at your palace, and there give their opinions; and that, your Grace's visitation approaching, you could then have the best opportunity of seeing what could be done in a matter of such consequence, as they seemed to think, to the woollen manufacture. But, instead of attending, as was expected, they came to me a fortnight after with a new proposal, that something should be written by an acceptable and able hand, to promote in general the wearing of home manufactures, and their civilities would fix that work upon me. I asked if they had prepared the stuffs, as they had promised, and your Grace expected; but they had not made the least step in the matter, nor as it appears, thought of it more."

I am not sure if we have even yet learned that the handling of a single rope to hoist a sail is more to the purpose of progress than any amount of whistling for a wind. Even if, however, the manufacturers had come into a plan suggested some years before by Swift to bind themselves "to sell the several sorts of stuffs, cloths and silks, made to the best perfection they were able for certain fixed prices, and in such a manner that, if a child were sent to any of their shops, the buyer might be secure of the value and goodness and measure of the ware," even then the venture ran the risk of wreck on many rocks. In the first place, it was as difficult then as it is now to persuade an Irish shop-keeper to sell, or an Irish customer to buy, native manufacture.

"I am convinced," writes Swift, in the same paper, "that if the virtuosi could once find out a world in the moon, with a passage to it, our women would wear nothing but what came directly from thence."

But, supposing Irish men, and even Irish women, resolved to wear only Irish stuffs, the very resolution bred a new danger—that the manufacturer, being thus secured in a monopoly, would with childish short-sightedness kill the goose that laid golden eggs.

"The mortal danger is that if these dealers could prevail by the goodness and cheapness of their cloths and stuffs to give a turn to the principal people of Ireland in favour of their goods, they would relapse into the knavish practice, peculiar to this kingdom, which is apt to run through all trades—adulteration and extortion."

It was such a crime and blunder that cost the country its lucrative linen trade with Spain.

"We have seen what a destructive loss the kingdom received by the detestable fraud of the merchants or northern linen weavers, or both—notwithstanding all the cares of the Governor of that Board, when we had an offer of commerce with the Spaniards for our linens to the value, as I am told, of £30,000 a year."

This tendency to discount the future for a small present advantage and

"To borrow joy at usury of pain,"

which is the tap-root of savagery, of much crime, and

of most vice is a necessary product of insecurity. We naturally, then, find it prevail most of all among those whose living was most precarious of all—the farmers.

> "Sic vos, non vobis, fertis aratra boves;
> Sic vos, non vobis, vellera fertis oves,"

because the oxen and sheep are, not higher, but lower, creatures than the farmer who works and fleeces them. The farmer whom a rack-renting landlord would similarly work and fleece, would deserve to be classed with these creatures, if he toiled only and incessantly and willingly for his griping master. But with the Irish tenant it was Hobson's choice. As there was nothing but the land to live by, the landlord, like the regrater of bread in a siege, could extort his own price; and his price was all that could be ground out of the soil less the few potatoes necessary to keep the tenant alive, and but alive. Even these few potatoes could often be procured in Swift's day only by begging and thieving, as in our own day, only by harvest labour in England. In a sermon on "The causes of the wretched condition of Ireland" Swift says:

> "A great cause of this nation's misery is that Egyptian bondage of cruel, oppressing, covetous landlords, expecting that all who live under them should make bricks without straw; who grieve and envy when they see a tenant of their own in a whole coat, or able to

afford one comfortable meal in a month; by which the spirits of the people are broken and made fit for slavery. The farmers and cottagers almost through the whole kingdom being, to all intents and purposes, as real beggars as any of those to whom we give our charity in our streets. And these cruel landlords are every day unpeopling the kingdom by forbidding their miserable tenants to till the earth, against common reason and justice, and contrary to the practice and prudence of all other nations, by which numberless families have been forced either to leave the kingdom, or stroll about and increase the number of our thieves and beggars."

Such a system would demoralize any people; and any people so demoralized for centuries can no more be regenerated in a moment by the charter of an Act of Parliament, than land so exhausted for centuries can in a moment be put into heart by the grant of a lease.

Let me give one more picture from Swift of this misery, tyranny and consequent demoralization. In a letter to the Dean of Emly he thus describes the state to which landlordism had reduced Tipperary.

"It is like the rest of the whole kingdom—a bare face of nature, without houses or plantations, filthy cabins, miserable, tattered, half-starved creatures, scarce in human shape. One ignorant, insolent, oppressive squire to be found in twenty miles' riding; a parish church to be found only in a summer day's journey, in comparison of which an English farmer's barn is a cathedral; a bog of fifteen miles around; every meadow a slough, and every hill a mixture of rock, heath, and marsh; and every male and female, from the farmer inclusive to the day-labourer, infallibly a thief, and consequently a beggar, which in this island are terms convertible."

Further on in the same letter he writes :—

"There is not an acre in Ireland turned to half its advantage, yet it is better improved than the people; and all these evils are the effects of English tyranny—so your sons and grand children will find to their sorrow."

Now during the whole of this stress of oppression and up even to to-day the English race and rulers and the Anglo-Irish landlords have taunted the Irish peasant with the very vices which English and landlord tyranny must have bred in angels. Oliver reproaching Orlando with being fit for nothing after he has done all he could to unfit him for anything! Since, however, the Irish peasant, like Orlando, has plucked up the spirit "to mutiny against this servitude," his moral advance in all the self-respecting virtues has been nothing less than astonishing, and Swift was the first to prescribe and to administer the tonic which has restored him his morale.

CHAPTER XIV.

SWIFT'S DETRACTORS.

"IRELAND is my debtor," said Swift, and she acknowledged the debt with ungrudging gratitude during his life. But since? Since, I fear, we have drawn from poisoned sources our impressions of our great benefactor. The writers from whom the popular impression of Swift has been derived, are uniformly and grossly unjust to him—Johnson, Jeffrey, Macaulay and Thackeray. But, it may be said, this unanimity, on one point, of men like Johnson and Macaulay, Jeffrey and Thackeray, who differ in all other points, is overpowering presumptive evidence against Swift. Not so, if all drew their impression from a single source, from the man who has given Swift the least deserving, and deserved, character of all—Swift himself. All misjudgments of Swift, other than those due to political prejudice, come from confounding the writer with the man. In every other case in literary history, perhaps, to look for an author's character in his works, as in a mirror, would be to find a far too flattering reflection; but in Swift's works, as in troubled water, we see a distorted image of the man. His case, in fact, was the precise converse of the proverbial one of Sterne's, whose practical humanity was in inverse proportion to his sentimental profession of philanthropy. "To love is to be lovely,' says Cowper, but the converse, "to hate is to be hateful," is not necessarily true, and was certainly not true in Swift's case; yet it is upon the assumption of its truth that his detractors have based their estimate of his character. So far, however, is this assumption from being true, that few men have been more loveable or more loved than Swift. Let us take up, for instance, Thackeray's foolish challenge, which, yet, is not the most foolish of all the spiteful things he says of Swift. "Would we have liked to live with him?" he asks in his lecture on Swift—surely an ill-judged challenge. The world never saw, says Thackeray himself, so brilliant a circle of wits as met together in that day, and of this circle Swift was the centre in right not only of his ability, but also of his sociability. And, he was supreme, remember, not only as a wit among wits, but as a statesman among statesmen.

Oxford, and the most brilliant of all the statesmen of that age, Bolingbroke, looked up to him for counsel as respectfully as Addison, Arbuthnot, Prior, Gay and Pope. But to be respected is not necessarily to be loved; nor, again, do sociability and amiability go together always. Swift, however, was loved, as he loved, tenderly and intensely; and those loved him most who lived most with him—Pope, Sheridan, Delany, and others. But the spirit in which Thackeray approached the subject of this lecture may be judged from the well-nigh incredible shallowness and woodenness of the following comment upon Swift's jesting advice to Gay to turn bishop.

"Take care of your health and your money," Swift writes to Gay, "Be less modest, more active, or else turn parson and get a bishopric here."

Upon this Thackeray, the humourist, makes the comment of an old Scotchwoman.

"I know of few things more conclusive as to the sincerity of Swift's religion than his advice to poor John Gay to turn clergyman and look out for a seat on the Bench. Gay, the author of the 'Beggar's Opera'; Gay, the wildest of the wits about town—it was this man that Jonathan Swift advised to take orders—to invest in a cassock and bands—just as he advised him to husband his shillings and put his thousand pounds out at interest."

"Flat burglary as ever was committed!" quoth Dogberry.

And what is this luckless little joke adduced to prove? That Swift was a hypocrite. Why, if Thackeray knew anything of Swift's life, he must have known that this hypocrite stole off daily to morning prayers when at the height of his power in London: that he read prayers daily to his servants so unostentatiously that Delany was six months in the Deanery before he became aware of this function: and that the prayers composed for Mrs. Esther Johnson on her death-bed breathe the most intense religious conviction.

Is it conceivable either, that Thackeray could have known of Swift's letter to Oxford on his fall, or of his correspondence with the family of Bolingbroke, when he had become the Secretary of the Pretender, and with Ormond when he had become the Pretender's General, and yet believe him to be a blustering coward?

"It is the first time," writes Swift to Oxford, begging to be allowed to attend him in the Tower on his fall. "It is the first time that I ever solicited you on my own behalf, and, if I am refused, it will be the first favour you ever refused me."

Could Thackeray have read or remembered Swift's dismissal of his butler when he was in Blakeney's power, and *because* he was in his power, and think the Dean a coward?

"I know that my life is in your power; and I shall not bear out of fear either your insolence or negligence."

How, again, any man unblinded by political partizanship can charge Swift, as Thackeray does, with having his pen and principles on sale, is to me inconceivable. As a matter of fact in a day of almost universal and shameless corruption Swift stood uncorrupted and incorruptible, towering as high morally as he did intellectually above most of his contemporaries. It is as difficult for historians as it is for painters to paint atmosphere, while their readers hardly ever allow environment its due effect upon the characters and careers of historical personages; yet it would be as unfair to judge a man without consideration of his environment, as it would be to pronounce a plant stunted or luxuriant without regard to its native climate or the clemency or inclemency of the season. Thus to appreciate duly the moral strength and purity of Swift's character, you must realize the foulness and infection of the air he breathed and of the surrounding corruption. I know no better way of attempting this in the short space at my command than that of taking an average man of Swift's position, profession, country and time, and comparing together their careers.

Here, then, is Dr. Theophilus Boulton, another Irish

Protestant divine, dignitary, and patriot who stood as high above the majority of his episcopal brethren as Swift stood above him. Upon Dr. Boulton's promotion to the See of Clonfert, Swift, in congratulating him, expressed the hope that the bishop, being an Irishman himself—a very exceptional thing in those days—would do what he could to further the interests of Ireland in the Irish House of Peers.

Dr. Boulton, however, pleaded that, as the bishopric was a poor one, and his promotion to a richer depended upon his keeping well with the Court, he could not yet afford to be a patriot.

"But, if you should get a better, you will then become an honest man?" urged Swift.

"That I will, Mr. Dean," replied the Bishop.

Upon his translation to Elphin, Swift reminded him of this promise—in vain. There was still to deflect the bishop from the path of patriotism the possibility of a promotion to an archbishopric. No sooner, however, had he attained this elevation than he waited on Swift to make to him the following naïve declaration:

"Mr. Dean, I am now at the top of my preferment, for I well know that no Irishman will ever be made Primate. Therefore, as I can rise no higher in fortune or station, I will zealously promote henceforth the good of my country."

And he did.

Here was an exceptionally worthy specimen of an Irish Church dignitary of that day, but how poor a creature does he look beside Swift.

"Miserable will be the condition of time-servers," says Fuller, "when their master is taken from them!" But "sufficient unto that day was the evil thereof" was the principle of the bulk of the Irish Protestant Hierarchy in Swift's time. They had their reward; and to suppose that a man of Swift's supreme power would have gone unrewarded, if his abilities and principles could have been purchased at any price is foolish. However, Thackeray's competency to lecture on Swift may be judged from his interpretation of that maddened cry against oppression—the "Modest Proposal"—as a mere exhibition of Swift's rage against children! probably the most shallow comment ever made on that terrible indictment of misgovernment. Indeed, Thackeray's lecture altogether would be below notice, if it had not unfortunately been the source from which the popular impression of Swift in our generation has been derived. His onslaught on Swift was, like Johnson's, inspired by personal antipathy, which may excuse prejudice, but not calumny. If you do not like Dr. Fell, cut him, but do not slander him; and Thackeray would have done better to keep clear of a subject to which he could not in any sense do justice.

For Jeffrey's and Macaulay's savage onslaughts on Swift, political prejudice is chiefly answerable.

Here is a single specimen of Jeffrey's truculent abuse:—" An apostate in politics, infidel or indifferent in religion, a defamer of humanity, the slanderer of statesmen who had served him, and destroyer of the women who loved him."

Jeffrey's venom, unlike Thackeray's, has long lost what little malignant power it had—a tiny blot of acrid ink which blackened himself more than Swift at the time, faded now to illegibility.

Macaulay's onslaught is of so much more consequence as he is so much more read; but all Macaulay's judgments have been by this so discredited that his readers now fortunately are on their guard. A judge who, like the prince in the fairy-tale, has but two alternatives to offer everyone brought before him—a throne or a block—necessarily gets to be suspected of weighting the scales of justice; and this Macaulay did habitually, influenced sometimes by prejudice, always by the love of startling effects. Hence Macaulay's "black and white style," which was the result of a precisely similar process to that by which the steward of the great Earl of Leicester stocked his preserves with black and white rabbits only.

"I should like in my warrens rabbits either all black or all white," ordered the Earl, and on his next visit he found his warrens almost depopulated owing to the steward's method of carrying out the order. By the simple process of eliminating all neutral-coloured rabbits he had contrived that the dozen or so which remained should be all either pure black or pure white. Similarly Macaulay's black and white is obtained by the elimination of all modifying or moderating facts, circumstances, or considerations.

To Swift he is even unusually and malignantly unfair. Contrasting him after this black and white fashion with Addison, he writes:—"In the front of the opposite ranks appeared a darker and a fiercer spirit—the apostate politician, the ribald priest, the perjured lover, a heart burning with hatred against the whole human race, a mind richly stored with images from the dung-hill and the lazar house."

All this because Swift with perfect consistency quitted the Whigs and their thrice-apostate Marlborough! Yet no one could read the life of Swift with any attention, but without any prepossession, and fail to see written in almost every line of it his incorruptible consistency.

"Only those," writes Scott in his *Life of Swift*, "who confuse principle with party and deem that consistency can only be claimed by such as with blindfold and undiscriminating attachment follow the banners and the leaders of a particular denomination of politicians," can deny that Swift " uniformly acted up to the two leading principles of his life "—the two principles being, support, on the one hand, of the Revolution, and, on the other, of the Church of England.

If Macaulay had read only *Gulliver's Travels*, he might not unfairly impute to Swift "a heart burning with hatred against the whole human race;" but he had read also the *Journal to Stella*, Bolingbroke's letters, and the letters of his literary idol, Addison. A more human and humane heart seldom beat than that whose every pulse we feel in the "Journal:" Bolingbroke, who lived in life-long and brotherly intimacy with Swift, writes:—"I love you for a thousand things." Addison, who, as we have seen describes Swift in his dedication to him of his *Travel, in Italy*, as "the most agreeable companion, the truest friend and the greatest genius of his age," says in a letter, that more even than for all these merits he honours him for his exceeding good nature and tenderness of heart. And even in her fury poor Vanessa makes this acknowledgment, "I know your good nature such that you cannot see any human creature miserable without being sensibly touched." Nor could he. He never left the Deanery without a pocketful of coppers for the beggars—in spite of his sound anti-mendicancy principles—while, in accordance with these principles, he kept £500 in the constant service of the industrious poor, which he lent out at £5 at a time for repayment at two shillings weekly. "You cannot imagine," testifies his house-keeper, Mrs. Brent, "what numbers of poor tradesmen, who have even wanted proper tools to carry on their work, have, by this small loan, been put into a prosperous way, and brought up their families in credit."

The most unworthy thing of many unworthy things in Johnson's *Life of Swift*, is his sneer at this mode of beneficence—perhaps the only form which does not feed the disease of mendicancy by abating a symptom. As for Swift's penuriousness—which also Johnson allows himself to sneer at, without remembering, what he of all men might well have remembered, that it had been bred into Swift's very bones by the bitterness of early dependence—it but subserved the Dean's generosity.

"The Dean," said Mrs. Brent, "hath found out a new method of being charitable, in which, however, I believe, he will have but few followers—which is, to debar himself of what he calls the superfluities of life, in order to administer to the necessities of the distressed. You just now saw an instance of it—the money a coach would have cost him he gave to a poor man unable to walk. When he dines alone, he drinks a pint of beer, and gives away the price of a pint of wine. And thus he acts in numberless instances."

Swift was infinitely above the imbecility of valuing money in and for itself—as though a manure-heap were an intrinsically desirable thing and not desirable only for the fruit and flowers producible through it. We should have been spared these unworthy sneers if Johnson had contrasted Swift's letters on the loss of friends with his letters on the loss of fortune. He was twice pecuniarily ruined by the ruin of friends. Of the bankruptcy of Stratford in 1712, which swallowed up Swift's entire fortune of £400, he writes thus to Stella:—

"I came home reflecting a little; nothing concerned me but M.D.. I called all my philosophy and religion up, and I thank God it did not keep me awake beyond my usual time, above a quarter of an hour."

Compare this with the letter to Stella on the stabbing of Harley, or that on the death of young Harrison, or that on the bereavement of the Duchess of Hamilton. Where in literature will you find deeper or tenderer sympathy expressed for mere and new friends?

"He that had a heart of that fine frame
To pay this debt of love but to a brother,"

was not tainted with inhumanity, least of all with the petty inhumanity of avarice.

In 1725 he writes thus to Sheridan of his second loss of fortune.

"You are to know that by Mr. Pratt's ruin I lose only twelve hundred and fifty pounds which he owes me. So that I am now, as near as I can compute, not worth one farthing but my goods. I am therefore just to begin the world. I should value it less if some friends and the public were not to suffer; and I am ashamed to see myself so little concerned on account of the two latter. For, as to myself, I have learned to consider what is left, and not what is lost. But enough of this."

Where was this philosophy, when his servant, Magee, died, at whose grave he wept so bitterly? Where was it, even when Sheridan himself, was being parted from him, not by death, but by distance? When Sheridan's house was being dismantled, preparatory to his removal to Cavan, Swift, unable to endure the sight of the disfurnishing of the parlour where he had passed so many happy hours with his friend, burst into tears, rushed into a dark closet, and had long to remain there before he could recover his composure.

The truth is that Johnson, Jeffrey, Macaulay, Thackeray and the other literary detractors of Swift have a human, beside, or apart from, a political, grudge against the author of *Gulliver's Travels*. "*Homo sum ; humani nihil a me alienum puto,*" and as a Whig can hardly be impartial toward a Tory, or a patriot toward a traitor to his country, so a man finds it difficult to forgive Gulliver his inhumanity. Hence, his detractors will not see that it was abstract and literary only and that few more "tender-hefted natures" than Swift's can be found among his contemporaries. Thus

"The evil that men do lives after them ;
The good is oft interred with their bones,"

when the good is personal and practical, but the evil impersonal and literary. It must, besides, be remembered that Swift differed from all other men of letters, not only in his scorn of fame—(with one slight exception, all his works were published anonymously) —but in his positive courtship of obloquy. He turned his back with savage scorn towards the world, and showed only his friends and the poor his heart. But those to whom alone he showed his heart are the best judges of its goodness, and by them Swift was loved as few men have ever been loved. Surely, these two considerations—Swift's anti-hypocritical affectation of brutality, and the love of all his intimates deepening with their intimacy—might have suggested to his posthumous maligners from Lord Orrery to Thackeray, that the man was as humane as the creator of the "Yahoos" and of the "Struldbrugs" was inhuman. I do not think I need ask my own people, who find so often that a rough tongue, a kind heart and a free and full hand go together among ourselves—that "sweetest nut hath sourest rind"—to forget Swift's words of scorn of the "natives," and remember only his championship of our cause, his tears as of blood for our sufferings, and his lonely and weary and hopeless, but Titanic, struggle for our deliverance.

CHAPTER XV.

"IRELAND IS MY DEBTOR."

T was a kind of Prometheus Vinctus sense of powerlessness in spite of all his power which inspired much of Swift's ferocity, and did much at last to break his heart. The savagery of the sardonic "Modest Proposal," for instance, is that of a tigress frenziedly tearing at the spear-shaft in her vitals in helpless agony of rage and pain. These horrors ever under his eye roused in him a sense at once of pity, of rage, and of mortified pride. All this suffering was horrible, was preventable, yet not a hand but his was outstretched to prevent it, and his was outstretched in vain. His proud spirit could not brook defeat, yet defeated he certainly was, not alone by Walpole and Boulter and England, but by Ireland herself. The success of the *Drapier's*

Letters agitation only made Walpole more merciless, and left Ireland more at his mercy. The country, as it has always done, and does still to-day, made a great effort only to sink back after it in exhaustion, apathy and despair; and neither Boulter's despotism nor Swift's appeals could stir it from its stupor. Swift had even condescended to apply to the Countess of Suffolk—the king's mistress, but the queen's tool, for in that swinish household the queen absolutely governed her husband through his mistress!—to this woman Swift also stooped to apply in his own interests, and in those of Ireland. "I wish," he writes to her, "Her Majesty would remember what I largely said to her about Ireland, when before a witness she gave me leave and commanded me to tell her what she had spoken to me on that subject, and ordered me, if I lived to see her in her present station, to send her our grievances, promising to read my letter, and to do all the good in her power for this miserable and loyal kingdom, now on the brink of ruin, and never so near as now." But from that day to this the House of Hanover has shrunk from Ireland as a rack-renting absentee shrinks from an estate which is a disgrace and reproach to him—always, and of course excepting her present Most Gracious Majesty, who has spent in our country twelve entire days during a reign of well-nigh sixty years.

Where else, then, could Swift look for help of hope? Only to Ireland herself, her Government and her Parliament, and these proved even rottener reeds to lean upon than the mistress of the king and of his kingdom. In 1734 Swift writes, "I have done some smaller services to this kingdom, but I can do no more. I have too many years upon me, and have too much sickness. I am out of favour at Court, where I was well received during two summers six or seven years ago. The governing people here do not love me; for, as corrupt as England is, it is a habitation of saints in comparison of Ireland. We are slaves and knaves and fools, and all but bishops and people in employment, beggars. The cash of Ireland does not amount to £200,000; the few honest men among us are dead-hearted, poor, and out of favour and power."

Thus Swift, in spite of his great powers and great efforts, had failed in everything, and in nothing more utterly, as it seemed, than in his single-handed struggle for the deliverance of Ireland. Can there be a doubt that the consciousness of what he was, the reflection of what he ought to have achieved for himself and for his country, and the contemplation of the comparatively beggarly result of all his life-long struggles, at once hastened and aggravated the malady which makes the last chapter of Swift's biography the most terrible reading in literary history?

For what more terrible spectacle is there in itself or in its suggestions than that of a great man who has survived himself; whose body but holds together the wrecks and ruins of his mind; and whose life, like the light in a Roman vault, shines only to show the piteous decay of mortality? Or, if there be anything more terrible—and it is so terrible that Dante makes it a torment of hell—it is the consciousness of all you have fallen from, haunting you in your fall. And this too, Swift had occasionally, if not continually, till he sank at last into the torpor of absolute imbecility. Such muttered groans as, "I am what I am," show his appalling consciousness of a great darkness that might be felt closing over him for ever, as waters over the drowning. And to this was superadded insupportable bodily agony. Not his brain only, but his whole body became violently inflamed, and the inflammation settling finally in one eye, caused him for weeks such torture that it needed all the strength of five young men to keep this old man of seventy-three from tearing his eye-ball from its socket. Nor was the cup full yet. The greatest genius of his age is at the last to lapse into idiocy, and its proudest spirit to be exhibited in its degradation as a show! After this last assault of physical torture, brain and body yielded together, leaving the enemy in possession of a shattered shell; and Swift for three years lived the life of

> "The fat weed
> That rots itself in ease on Lethe wharf."

In this condition he was on show, for payment, to strangers! The hackneyed lines of Johnson were literally true :—

> "In life's last scene what prodigies surprise!
> Fears of the brave, and follies of the wise!
> From Marlborough's eyes the streams of dotage flow,
> And Swift expires a driveller and a show!"

Those who saw Swift, before madness sank into imbecility, as a flame goes out in smoke, pacing ceaselessly and unapproachably his study, his very meals left for him to devour unwatched—as for a savage beast newly caught and caged—witnessed only the full and final development of a lifelong disorder. The appalling spectacle of a mind so noble so o'erthrown pleads in mitigation of the harsh judgments measured out to him, and on grounds more rational than those of mere pity. For surely this daemonic spirit, which so rent and tore him when it was being finally driven out, must have possessed him all his life through, inspiring that fell rage against man, which has raised every man's hand against the creator of the Yahoo. Those who witnessed Swift's insane and ceaseless pacing of his den, were witnessing, in fact, a revelation similar to that made to Vathek by Soliman in the Halls of Eblis, when the prophet, raising for a moment his hands toward heaven, disclosed through his bosom, which was transparent as crystal, a heart enveloped in flames. This, then, was the frightful reason that each baleful spectre, hiding ever his heart with his hand, wandered lonely in a crowd, homeless in a palace, and tormented, " like a tiger wounded with a poisoned arrow," by insatiate and insensate rage. Swift had gone through life as these doomed souls through the Halls of Eblis, hiding a heart in flames, which were unveiled at its close, showing his misanthropy to be a disease claiming pity, and not *lèse majesté* against human nature deserving vindictive reprobation.

Let it not be forgotten, either, and least of all forgotten in Ireland, that Swift's misanthropy was abstract—hate of man, not of men—and that its concrete form was the noblest which hatred can assume—rage against injustice and oppression. But it is not possible for Irishmen to forget this, since it stands on record—and it is all that is recorded—in the epitaph in St. Patrick's composed by Swift himself. Looking back upon a life memorable for many and great things, he cares to be remembered for one thing alone—his strenuous struggle for Irish freedom. He gave in his will precise instructions, which were carried out to the letter, that he was to be buried privately at dead of night in the cathedral, and that on a tablet of black marble, in large letters, "deeply cut and strongly gilded," was to be engraved this epitaph :—

"HIC DEPOSITUM EST CORPUS,
JONATHAN SWIFT, S.T.P,
HUJUS ECCLESIAE CATHEDRALIS
DECANI:
UBI SAEVA INDIGNATIO
ULTERIUS COR LACERARE NEQUIT.
ABI VIATOR
ET IMITARE SI POTERIS
STRENUUM PRO VIRILI LIBERTATIS VINDICEM
OBIIT ANNO (1745)
MENSIS (OCTOBRIS) DIE (19)
AETATIS ANNO (78)."

Johnson also in his *Life of Swift*, where he extenuates nothing, but sets much down in unaccountable malice, thinks his service to Ireland the chief distinction of his life.

"In the reign of Queen Anne he turned the stream of popularity against the Whigs, and must be confessed to have dictated for a time the policy of the English nation. In the succeeding reign he delivered Ireland from plunder and oppression; and showed that wit, confederated with truth, had such force as authority was unable to resist. He said truly of himself that 'Ireland was his debtor.' It was from the time that he first began to patronise the Irish that they date their riches and prosperity. He taught them first to know their own interest; their weight and strength, and gave them spirit to assert that equality with their fellow-subjects, to which they have ever since been making vigorous advances, and to claim those rights which they have at last established. Nor can they be charged with ingratitude to their benefactor; for they reverenced him as a guardian, and obeyed him as a dictator.'

It is, in fact, incontestable that Swift's service to Ireland deserves the distinction he gives it in his epitaph. Look at it how you will, either from the point of view of the need of the service, or of its righteousness, or of its greatness, or of its difficulty, and Swift's work in Ireland is his supreme achievement. When " in the reign of Queen Anne he dictated for a time the policy of the English nation," he had at his back a powerful and compact party, all the influence (then enormous) of the Court, Harley's serviceable cunning and the brillant intellect of Bolingbroke. But of his work in Ireland he might say with literal truth, "Alone I did it!" All England, Court and Ministry, parties and people, were solid against him; solid against him also was a nearer, fiercer and fouler enemy, the Irish Government and Judiciary, murderous and remorseles as hired bravos; but at his back, no one! The spirit of the Irish people—" the aborigines "—had fainted within them under insupportable oppression and misery, while the currish spirit of the "colonists" cringed to England's heel at a word. If there was a single sensitive spot about them it lay in their breeches pocket, yet the "Proposal for the Universal Use of Irish Manufacture," addressed exclusively to this susceptible region, was incriminated by two colonist Grand Juries as "a seditious, factious and virulent libel."

Here was stuff as promising as those recruits of Clive's who fled at the first report of one of their own guns; yet to the same men in a few months the strongest French fortress in India capitulated. Not less astonishing was the spirit to which Walpole capitulated, breathed by Swift in a few months into hearts as craven. He had declared war without a single soldier behind him, and then, as it were with a stamp of his foot, he had raised an army out of the ground and led it to victory. The victory was not final; what, on the contrary, seemed final was the subsequent defeat and prostration of the country under the heel of Archbishop Boulter; but almost every great teacher, secular or sacred, in history has had to pay the price of present failure for the future and final success of his principles.

The greatest of teachers is the farthest in advance of his time; and to be far in advance of your time is the greatest of crimes. Thus the arch-malefactors of yesterday are the saints of to-day, and we build the sepulchres of the Prophets our fathers had stoned. It is not the extravagant compliment it seems, to rank Swift with the Prophets who were defeated in their life-time and because of their greatness, only to triumph finally, through the spirit and the doctrine they bequeathed; for politically and in Ireland he was the Moses of his day. If he left his people in the Wilderness he showed them the way out of Egypt and the way into Canaan. To his example Ireland owes— and it is no small debt—her Protestant leaders, Lucas, Flood, Grattan and Parnell; to his initiative she owes the system of inert, dogged and solid resistance to oppression; and to his teaching she owes the lessons, that we must be self-respecting to be respected, self-reliant to be prosperous and self-dependent to be free. But of all the noble and needed exhortations he has addressed to us, that of his epitaph makes on us the most urgent, exacting and heroic demand:—

IMITARE SI POTERIS

STRENUUM PRO VIRILI LIBERTATIS VINDICEM

THE STORY OF EARLY GAELIC LITERATURE.

BY

DOUGLAS HYDE, LL.D.

NEW IRISH LIBRARY, Vol. VI.

NOTICES OF THE PRESS.

"The story of 'Early Gaelic Literature' is the title of the latest work added to the rapidly growing series of the New Irish Library. The author is Dr. Douglas Hyde, and the book, though issued in an unpretentious form by Mr. T. Fisher Unwin is of the rarest interest to every student of Irish literature. . . . Books like that of Dr. Hyde are lights in the van of advancement."
—IRISH TIMES, March 8th, 1895. *Leading article on the book.*

"Dr. Hyde has the ideal scholarly qualities, the patience, the enthusiasm, the research, the love of his work, and he has in addition the power of placing before us the knowledge he has collected with a literary skill and charm that lift his work out of the category of the specialist. . . . We hope this addition to the New Irish Library will sell by tens of thousands in Ireland. It is informed with more knowledge, sympathy, and power of imparting knowledge that many rich tomes on the shelves of wealthy collectors and in college libraries. A rich shilling's-worth! It makes us thirsty for more yet to come from this fountain-head."—DAILY INDEPENDENT. *Leading article on the book*, March 15th, 1895.

"One could not have a pleasanter or a more accomplished guide to the beauties of the treasure-house of Irish poetry and romance. His translations, while preserving as much as possible of the colour, style, and even accent of the original, are excellently done, and are in themselves good literature."—FREEMAN'S JOURNAL, March 17th, 1895.

"Those who read the Story of Early Gaelic Literature should not omit to read its preface, for it is one of the most remarkable parts of a remarkable book. . . . The Story of Early Gaelic Literature is a book of which every Irishman, no matter what his creed may be, should feel proud. It is a noble work on a noble theme, and it is to be hoped its gifted author will produce many more like it."—DAILY EXPRESS, March 21st, 1895.

"To the true Celtic Irishman it will be as wine to warm his blood, one of the noblest vindications ever penned of the learning, the genius, and the civilization of the far-scattered, but indestructable race of the Clanna-Gael."—UNITED IRELAND, March 30th, 1895.

"In the Story of Early Gaelic Literature is given to the public a book which we trust no Irishman pretending to interest in national matters will neglect to read. . . . Dr. Hyde set before himself what to him is a pleasant task, and he has fulfilled it in a manner beyond all praise."—EVENING TELEGRAPH, March 9th, 1895.

Preparing for Immediate Publication

A FINAL EDITION
OF
YOUNG IRELAND.

A FRAGMENT OF IRISH HISTORY 1842-1846.

Illustrated with Portraits, Autographs, Facsimilies and Historical Scenes.

BY THE
Hon. Sir C. GAVAN DUFFY, K.C.M.G.

To be published in two parts, 2s. each, largely illustrated, and in a volume handsomely bound, price 5s.

OPINIONS OF THE CRITICAL PRESS.

From the Saturday Review.

"The party which Davis created, and of which Duffy took the leadership from his hand, had many engaging characteristics, and these characteristics had never been so effectively set out before. The author abstained to a great extent from that curse of Irish controversy— indiscriminate and personal abuse of those who differed with him. The reception of Young Ireland was thus favourable even with those who could least admit its author's political postulates, or arrive at his historical standpoint. It was recognized as a valuable contribution to history where the author spoke with personal knowledge, and an interesting contribution to literature even where he did not."

From THE TIMES.

"The gifted and ill-fated Party of Young Ireland certainly deserved an APOLOGIA, and it is past dispute that no one could be more competent for the task than Sir Charles Gavan Duffy. Notwithstanding the genuine modesty with which he always attributes the origin of the school (for, in the true sense, it was a school rather than a party) to Thomas Davis, he will, we think, be always regarded as its true founder. He established and guided from 1842 to 1855 the NATION, which was in those days its one accepted organ. A State prisoner with O'Connell in 1844, with Smith O'Brien in 1848, three times tried, and all but convicted of treason in 1848, he organized, after his release from prison, a peaceful agitation for the measures which afterwards formed the main achievements of Mr. Gladstone's Irish policy. Proceeding to Australia in 1855, he has been some time Prime Minister of Victoria and Speaker, and while he filled the chair it is said order reigned in that tumultuous Parliament."

From THE EDINBURGH REVIEW.

"These, it seems, were the founders, heroes, and martyrs of the NATION, and we are free to confess that the Young Ireland of those days had incomparably more patriotism, eloquence, and energy than their degenerate successors. But even Ireland cannot produce an inexhaustible supply of Davises and Duffys. It is in the nature of all human things:—

'In pejus ruere et retro sublapsa referri.'"

www.ingramcontent.com/pod-product-compliance
Lightning Source LLC
Chambersburg PA
CBHW020826230426
43666CB00007B/1110